DATE DUE

APR 2 3 2007			
JUL 1 6 2007			

Demco, Inc. 38-293

Defensive Measures

Defensive Measures

The Poetry of Niedecker, Bishop, Glück, and Carson

Lee Upton

Lewisburg
Bucknell University Press

Associated University Presses
2010 Eastpark Boulevard
Cranbury, NJ 08512

The paper used in this publication meets the requirements of the American National Standard for Permanence of Paper for Printed Library Materials Z39.48-1984.

Library of Congress Cataloging-in-Publication Data

Upton, Lee, 1953–
    Defensive measures : the poetry of Niedecker, Bishop, Glück, and Carson / Lee Upton.
        p.   cm.
    Includes bibliographical references and index.
    ISBN 0-8387-5607-7 (alk. paper)
    1. American poetry—20th century—History and criticism.   2. Women and literature—United States—History—20th century.   3. American poetry—Women authors—History and criticism.   4. Bishop, Elizabeth, 1911–1979—Criticism and interpretation.   5. Glück, Louise, 1943—Criticism and interpretation.   6. Carson, Anne, 1950—Criticism and interpretation.   7. Niedecker, Lorine—Criticism and interpretation.   I. Title.

PS151.U68   2005
811'.5099287—dc22   2004062343

for Cecilia

Contents

Acknowledgments

I am grateful to Lafayette College and its provost, June Schlueter, for an enhanced sabbatical during which most of this book was written.

Special thanks to Greg Clingham, director of Bucknell University Press, for his support of my work, and to Malcolm Hayward, editor of *Studies in the Humanities*, who first published my writing about Elizabeth Bishop. I am also grateful to Julien Yoseloff and Christine A. Retz of Associated University Presses.

The staff of Skillman Library has long been greatly helpful, and I want to express my gratitude to the director, Neil McElroy.

I am deeply indebted to Jill Riefenstahl, our admirable administrative assistant in the English Department of Lafayette College.

Special thanks to the following for their support: Susan Blake, Carla Beers, Anna Duhl, Alexis Fisher, Bill Osborn, Diane Shaw, Carolynn Van Dyke, and Sylvia Watanabe.

Although I'm writing about defense, Theodora and Cecilia Ziolkowski have no need of any defense whatsoever; they are beyond perfection. Rose Upton has enriched our lives immeasurably by joining our household permanently. Finally, as always, I thank Eric Ziolkowski for unsurpassed integrity and imagination—and for kindness beyond measure.

Grateful acknowledgment is made to individuals and publishers who gave permission to reprint copyrighted material.

Excerpts from GLASS, IRONY AND GOD, by Anne Carson, copyright © 1922, 1994, 1995 by Anne Carson. Reprinted by permission of New Directions Publishing Corporation.

"Poetry" reprinted with the permission of Scribner, an imprint of Simon & Schuster Adult Publishing Group, from THE COLLECTED POEMS OF MARIANNE MOORE by Marianne Moore. Copyright © 1935 by Marianne Moore; copyright renewed © 1963 by Marianne Moore and T. S. Eliot.

Excerpts from THE COMPLETE POEMS: 1927–1979 by Elizabeth Bishop. Copyright © 1979, 1983 by Alice Helen Methfessel. Reprinted by permission of Farrar, Straus and Giroux, LLC.

Portions from "Through the Lens of Edward Lear: Contesting Sense in the Poetry of Elizabeth Bishop," by Lee Upton, *Studies in the Humanities* 19.1 (1992): 68–79. Reprinted by permission of Malcolm Hayward, Editor, *Studies in the Humanities*.

Excerpts from THE SEVEN AGES by Louise Glück, copyright © 2001 by Louise Glück. Reprinted by permission of HarperCollins Publishers Inc.

Excerpts from THE FIRST FOUR BOOKS OF POEMS by Louise Glück, copyright 1968, 1971, 1972, 1973, 1974, 1975, 1976, 1977, 1978, 1979, 1980, 1985, 1995 by Louise Glück. Reprinted by permission of HarperCollins Publishers Inc.

Excerpts from *Lorine Niedecker: Collected Works*, edited by Jenny Lynn Penberthy, copyright © 2002 The Regents of the University of California. Reprinted by permission of the Regents of the University of California.

Defensive Measures

Introduction: Poetry as Defense

Poetry is the literary form that incites defense. Perpetually in crisis over matters of its utility, or its dismissal of utility, its aesthetic appeal, or its renunciation of such an appeal, its generic existence, or its rebuke to the conceit of genre, poetry courts high expectations and, often enough, dashes them. Surely Plato's challenge to anyone who might defend poetry against perpetual exile on charges of its infective and imitative qualities has not stopped resonating: "Shall I propose, then, that she be allowed to return from exile, but upon this condition only—that she make a defence of herself in some lyrical or other metre?"[1] Poetry needs its defenders, not only for its forays against prior aesthetic convention in each new generation, but as the genre whose every particular is held up for examination as symptomatic of the culture from which it emerges (and, ironically, as such, poetry may be deplored for even its unwitting absorption of cultural convention).

As Wallace Stevens wrote, "All poetry is experimental poetry."[2] Surely it is not farfetched to say that experiment, by its nature, invites attack. Poetry's defenders have their work cut out for them. While the novel is said by some every few decades to be dying, poetry is most frequently defending itself and claiming its own resuscitation. Consider the tenor of even a brief selection of the arguments arising from some of the more well-known defenses of poetry in English. Whatever reasoning is advanced in poetry's defense, the defender's tone has often been one of exaltation, even when threads of irony may be shot through the rhetoric of uplift. Poetry is, among other things, a vehicle for praise in Sidney's defense/apology, closing with the famous curse, that the recalcitrant reader's "memory [may] die from the earth for want of an epitaph."[3] If we turn to Shelley's defense, poetry is not only the master work of "unacknowledged legislators" but must illuminate and refine: "We want the creative faculty to imagine that which we know; we want the generous impulse to act that which we imagine;

13

we want the poetry of life: our calculations have outrun conception; we have eaten more than we can digest."[4] In Emerson's formulation "Poets are . . . liberating gods."[5] Walter Pater defends poetry as a heightening of our responsiveness to the business of living: "for art comes to you professing frankly to give nothing but the highest quality to your moments as they pass, and simply for those moments' sake."[6] W. H. Auden is drawn to a defensive strategy in which the poet justifies a celebratory art: "Whatever its actual content and overt interest, every poem is rooted in imaginative awe. Poetry can do a hundred and one things, delight, sadden, disturb, amuse, instruct—it may express every possible shade of emotion, and describe every conceivable kind of event, but there is only one thing that all poetry must do; it must praise all it can for being and for happening."[7] As Lucy McDiarmid asserted in *Auden's Apologies for Poetry*, "Only in the imagination of an imagined deity live the poems that do not need apology."[8]

Somewhat drier arguments have surely been put in service of the art. (Even the Dadaists were not exempt from defending at least their refusal to defend poetry. Tristan Tzara in 1918 felt compelled to claim, "I am neither for nor against and I do not explain because I hate common sense.")[9] Dana Gioia's *Can Poetry Matter*, appearing first as an essay in May 1991 in *The Atlantic*, offers a diagnosis of contemporary poetry's troubles with its current audience, a defense of poetry as a genre, and a tentative prescription for its revival. The essay, turned into a book and ten years later into a new edition with a new foreword, generated copious commentary, as if to exemplify the suggestion that defenses of poetry do not stabilize—a notion which Marianne Moore's defense of poetry makes clear even in its publication history. The tone of understatement that animates defenses that forego uplift is perhaps most famously employed in "Poetry":

> I, too, dislike it.
>   Reading it, however, with a perfect contempt for it, one dis-
>   covers in
>   it, after all, a place for the genuine.[10]

The poem itself, in the severely excised form that Moore approved for its publication in *Complete Poems*, prompts an occasion for defense. She knew her decision to cut over two dozen lines would be met with disagreement. She acknowledges her readers' likely bafflement with the collection's prefatory note: "Omissions are not accidents." She makes a defense of poetry that itself must be defended not only for readers familiar with the earlier version of the poem, but for readers familiar with more directly vigorous defenses of poetry. As such, she firmly counters our expectations of what constitutes a defense. Certainly "Poetry" as a defense of the art appears camouflaged as a lukewarm apology—and as an occasion for questions: Why, after all, should we be attentive to what we dislike? Why submit to poetry, under this definition, unless under the compunction of duty? For Moore, it is significant that contempt for poetry can be "perfect." The poem's discriminating speaker feigns an initial disdain only to inoculate us with the germ of disapproval. In poetry, she argues, one finds not only "the genuine" but "a place for the genuine." Her argument is then, in some measure, about positioning. To continue with her argument by illustration within the poem, to exemplify further with multiple examples as does the original version of the poem, may appear to spoil the game after the battle is won. She allows the newly abbreviated poem to resonate in the context of the volume, a volume which provides ample illustration of the qualities that she introduced in the poem's earlier versions. As such, she suggests, poetry becomes itself through context; poetry is poetry by virtue of the place it inhabits.

We often think of individual poems as engaged in offensive measures, as putting forward imagistic assertions and wresting a position, however deeply ambiguous that position may be. We may look at the way a poem accedes to or challenges its aesthetic, cultural, and historical context. Yet most, if not all, poems of worth supply us with not only offensive strikes, but defensive ones as well. To write poetry is to foreground a practice that may at least accommodate some forms of defensive measures as well as offensive measures. According to the *OED*, defense is "the action of warding off, and of prohibiting"; "the action of keeping off, or resisting the attack"; "the action of guarding or protecting from attack." A "line of defense" refers to "a line or series of fortified points at which an enemy is resisted." Poetry, I want to argue, is the language of defense as much as the language of the offensive measure—that is, poetry would seem to have mechanisms for shielding, even of re-

treating, as much as it contains or exemplifies measures of asser-
tion. As Charles Bernstein claims, poetry can be rooted in some
aspects of "aversion": *"Poetry is aversion of conformity* in the pursuit
of new forms, or can be."[11]

Many poems, particularly contemporary poems, occupy at least
a partially defensive position, warding off immediate understand-
ing in a way that draws upon early modernist experiments which
have conditioned poets' and readers' responses. Such poems may
be fortified not only by markers of innovation and the "difficulty"
that T. S. Eliot among others espouses, but by defensive measures
that would seem implicit in the art. To engage a poem is to enter a
rhythm and gather physical energy, but to do so means that some
other habits of mind and perception may be frustrated. To disas-
semble, to double, are mechanisms common to many contempo-
rary poems. A way to approach the situation: a poet's defensive
strategies serve to keep readerly rigidity and fixedness at bay. The
situation is exemplified in Emily Dickinson's "The Soul selects her
own Society—" in which the soul operates as a valve.[12] A valve may
shut off entry and alternately open for entry. The image of "The
Valves of . . . attention" in Dickinson's poem suggests that poetry
may allow us into the experience of feeling and conceiving but may
also defend against other sorts of appropriation. Wallace Stevens's
claim that "Poetry must resist the intelligence almost successfully"
suggests something along the order of defense as well; a poem may
not be had too cheaply—a certain sort of poem requires the mech-
anisms of its own resistance to counter desensitized conceptions.
After all, if a poem appears adamantly self-conscious and assured
of all its mechanisms, it may not prove to be a poem of significant
dynamism. Seemingly such a self-consistent poem cannot enact
movement *toward* knowledge, the "play of mind" that Charles
Olson, for one, celebrates.[13] We tend to respect what constitutes
degrees of difference: the poem of resistance that offers us another
way of seeing through, alongside, or into states of experience, in-
cluding the experience of language. Poems must be engaged by
the reader, but not so readily that the reader perceives the poem
as depleted. That is, we respond to poetry that through some
mechanism defeats easy assimilation not only by the readers' un-
derstanding but by assimilation into the field of other poems. A
poem is no longer vital when it is indistinguishable from other
poems of its period and culture, and we can no longer ascertain its

individuality. At best such a poem is representative and serves as an illustration. As Harold Bloom asserts, "Defense, for poets, always has been trope, and always has been directed against prior tropes."[14] In Bloom's well-known narrative, the struggle of succession through misreading is related to the poet's ability to manipulate style as defense. Even poets often cast as personally self-effacing conduct a struggle with their contemporaries as well as their poetic ancestors. Style is both a weapon and a shield.

It is my argument that much of our strongest contemporary poetry written in English learned its lessons through early modernism and lives by its defensive measures, that is, by reversing, inverting, or challenging in overt or covert ways a dominant perceptual mode. Here I wish to consider defense in poetry by looking at how poems create the illusion of a certain "distance" between poem and reader, and between poem and ostensible subject. Looking at defensive moments may seem to be looking at offenses in disguise—but there is a difference. Defensive measures insist on difference. Poems defend themselves, even many of the inviting, seemingly open poems of spontaneity, by setting up a bounded quality that allows us to recognize the poem's features, its means of delineating linguistic experience. Poems ask, that is, to be recognized, but to be recognized requires a distinguishing membrane. The urge toward defense, the outlining of a boundary path, the channel the poem makes or the pattern upon which it rides, requires our conception of an intervening skin. Even as a poem may dip in and out of other genres, it returns to find a shape and a recurrent sonic effect. The most seemingly unarmored and inclusive poem venturing forward with the pennants of an anaphoric style waving must glide over the opposition, netting particulars and pulling us after. A poem makes its own material conditions. It must have designs that are bold and designs that are hidden. And yet poetry puts up provisional defenses, not final ones. "'No' is the wildest word," Emily Dickinson wrote, and is often quoted approvingly for having written so. Defensive measures echo her estimation.

Defense, I have to admit, is a problematic conception. For one thing, it would seem essentially reactive, antithetical to the image of the experimentalist breaking the gates of custom. A poetry of defenses would seem to be, then, a poetry that blocks experience and reduces frames of reference. We have only to call up the most rudimentary conception of the Freudian defense mechanism to see the problem, for a poetry of defense would appear to be a querulous poetry of repression, blocking inclusiveness and vitality. While I am not working with a Freudian model of defense, it is necessary that we draw at least a tentative link. As Margaret Ferguson argues in describing a Freudian conception of defense, "the defense can best be described as a 'boundary creature'—a metaphor Freud uses to describe the ego."[15] As Ferguson emphasizes, Freud links defense to repression; our defenses allow us to hide from ourselves whatever would threaten our better estimates of ourselves. Ferguson claims, "Defenses generally occur as responses to threats which may be seen as coming from an 'external world,' and they also characteristically employ a 'rhetoric of motives' to express wishes and fears that may be said to come from within the authorial psyche."[16]

Here I want to argue that defense in a poem is not passive but requires capacity, a readiness to insulate and withdraw to create a marker of difference. The sort of poetry that I have found particularly inventive arrives in a crust of sort, with a set of conventions, a relation to duration and a capacity to enact differences. To survive the journey as a poem that will be read into the future it must contain itself and transmit itself, as a valve of sorts in the way that Dickinson used the term. A deeply realized poem tends to project a realm of defensive control and another of compulsion.

Defense is figured in this book in at least three ways; as distance itself, as the representation of, or the dramatization of, a gulf of some sort between author and reader and reader and poem; as figurings of reversals and distortions of imagery that repel the readers' possession of the poem; and as the act of inscribing borders or boundaries in space. Questions about defense ask what is bounded in the poem: What is protected? What is contracted and withheld? How does the poem avoid or court "contamination"—or immersion in other forms and genres, and when does the poem retract from its investment in other genres?

Two assumptions animate my argument: poems have something to defend—their form and their way of knowing/unfolding, particularly given that poetry is the genre most intricately linked to physicality and to bodily articulation, to materializing words with heightened attention to sound devices and patterns of silence. My second point is that the defensive measures that a poet chooses are an integral part of the poem and the means by which we at least intermittently recognize the poem as poetry. That is, defense leads to identification.

To think of defense at all means usually to imagine spatially in some way, and thus to consider the poem as constituting territory. Perhaps the habit of spatializing is particularly heightened in terms of poetry. Poetry as a genre may be readily experienced in terms of the problematics of an "inside" and an "outside." Because often poems are thought of as "compressed and condensed" language, as fretted with meaning, it is common to endow poems with metaphors that allude to their holding greater amounts of conceptual material in less space than do other forms of writing, and accordingly poems may be viewed metaphorically as carriers or conductors. A focus on condensing language in poetry may also lead us to think about poems as creating the illusion of interiority; as the derivation of the very word *stanza* itself (room, "halting place") becomes literalized for us. It is indeed very difficult to think of poetry without thinking at some point in spatial terms, even if we metaphorize poems as "husks,"[17] as does Bernstein, for even a husk often retains some shapely indication of its former contents.

In *The Incarnate Word: Literature as Verbal Space,* Cary Nelson refers to "space" as "inherent to literary form" and refers to spatiality as "a critical and perceptual tool." He goes so far as to argue that "Pure spatiality is a condition toward which literature aspires, but which it never achieves."[18] He stipulates "verbal form as an author's projection of a self-protective and self-generative space that transcends or escapes historical time."[19] While Nelson has focused on "a dialogue with history" increasingly in recent years, his early position that "identification with verbal space . . . may temporarily free us from the impulse toward historical assimilation"[20] remains vital, for the pleasures poems offer have to do in large measure with our apprehension of their shapes and our relation to such shapes in time. A poem may be experienced as a surrounding in which we position ourselves. Or we may consider poems as designed to operate like objects in a small area or to be deployed as a process across a field, as in Charles Olson. We focus on open and closed structures, or alternately opening and closing circuits. We are concerned with how the poem enacts or escapes stasis, or how it handles internal interruptions of the conceptual field it first establishes. In turn we may think of the poem as procedural, moving outward, projecting words and as such meeting the reader or, in turn, being put into action by the reader. Even the most declamatory poem may suggest a progression outward from an inwardness of some sort. As William Carlos Williams advised, we may "think with the poem," but we find ourselves thinking over and with and into the poem by virtue of the etymology of words, given that they pull us along an axis which we may conceptualize in metaphor as striking through an interior.

In his lineated essay "Articles of Absorption," Bernstein refers to "artifice" as "a measure of a poem's / intractability to being read as the sum of its / devices & subject matter."[21] He delineates the key strategies of absorption as follows:

> By *absorption* I mean engrossing, engulfing
> completely, engaging, arresting attention, reverie,
> attention intensification, rhapsodic, spellbinding,
> mesmerizing, hypnotic, total, riveting,
> enthralling: belief, conviction, silence.
>
> *Impermeability* suggests artifice, boredom,
> exaggeration, attention scattering, distraction,
> digression, interruptive, transgressive,
> undecorous, anticonventional, unintegrated, fractured,
> fragmented, fanciful, ornately stylized, rococo,
> baroque, structural, mannered, fanciful, ironic,
> iconic, schtick, camp, diffuse, decorative,
> repellent, inchoate, programmatic, didactic,
> theatrical, background muzak, amusing: skepticism,
> doubt, noise, resistance.[22]

My own focus on defensive measures allows that the strategies/feeling-states that Bernstein defines as either absorptive or impermeable may cross one another readily. One poet may keep at bay a prevailing cultural style by incorporating measures from either listing that Bernstein supplies. The poem that engulfs and absorbs readers may have defended itself from aesthetic appropriation because of its very capacity to seduce and baffle. By contrast, the poem of artifice or exaggeration may not have defended its boundaries; in some cases, it is easily assimilated into a dominant means of perceiving, its mechanisms apparently mastered. Thus defense, as I am constituting it, is more about textual effects in contexts of asserting difference. The poem may be invested with shield or shell as necessary and even as a mark of growth—of calcifying a part of itself, all the better to enact a defense and impede absorption by any single aesthetic convention of reading.

It seems inevitable that defense is allied to our conceptions of distance. To defend is to keep something or someone at a distance. In Old French *distant* means "standing apart" and refers to "separation, opening (between): distance; remoteness; difference; diversity." Distance conveys the meaning of "discord, quarrel." The first definition the *OED* provides for distance is "the condition of being at variance." As such, the spatial term *distance* is linked from its early developments with human feeling and social station. The word's etymological connection to quarrels and combat is connected to the spatial, "The fact or condition of being apart or far off in space; remoteness." Human relationships are figured in measurements of space, applied to "remoteness or degree of remoteness." In turn, differences between people are linked to one's social status, "arising from disparity of rank or station, or exclusiveness of feeling." Thus we have the phrases "to keep one's distance" and "to know one's distance."

Defense depends on establishing distance, a boundary, and as such defense is most recognizable as a device that creates the illusion of distance. Significantly, questions of defense nearly always are inflected with questions of distance. How "close" are we to the poem? How seemingly intimate and reliable is the poem's speaker prepared to be with the reader? (A speaker, once establishing that he or she is unreliable, after all, can be "reliably unreliable"; so much depends upon the rules that the poem first makes.) The strategies of representing or enacting the sensation of experiencing distance may occur through presentations of holding others at bay, psychologically and physically, and may take the form of repeated scenes of departure; enacting moments of misunderstanding and thus of intellectual and emotional dislocation; creating dimensions of spatial removal; poising the poem against common conceptions of intimacy; returning to initiating moments of perceived disagreement; enacting sudden irruptions of geographical distance; or representing diagrams or landscapes that allow us to calculate physical distance.

By now it seems that we ought to ask, How is a conception of defense useful to us? My answer is that the concept is useful when pliable, particularly if we consider defensive measures in poetry as mechanisms for keeping the poem from fading entirely into other aesthetic fields. The things we don't do for one another are infinite; the things a poem refuses to do cannot be numbered either. We do not often look at poems in terms of negation; it seems even rather unfair to the projections a poem makes. What's done, what's accomplished, is more often our focus. Nevertheless, every poem works along pathways of choices and commitments. No poem appeals to everyone, not even to everyone of either the angel's or the devil's party. Bringing awareness to the ways a poem closes certain valves while opening others allows us to trace along the language of a poem for particular textures, speculating on what might have been a likely path and what path might have been abandoned. Especially when looking at "problem" poems, poems that seem curiously inhospitable to analysis, we may gain insight into ranges of experience that the poems turn from as well as ranges of experience the poems embrace. We ask: What are a poem's sins of omissions and its points of neglect? In *Toy Medium* Daniel Tiffany advances the position, "To pursue the question of the nature of lyric substance would require close attention to the kind of body produced by lyric; to the nature of its material substance, whether continuous or discontinuous, palpable or impalpable; to its modes of appearance and disappearance; to its limits, its temporal nature, and its modes of relation."[23] A defense, as I will argue, may be terminable and fragile, but it nevertheless must point to a separation, a recognition of limits. A poem may attempt to exceed its limits— but once a limit is exceeded a new limit is established. As such, by considering defensive measures we are taking pleasures in the withdrawn, the buried, the resistant. Considering defense, of course, opens up more questions than we can begin to explore here, including how poems accommodate or resist their cultures of origin and how they may be marked by the rhetoric of national defense during the modern and contemporary periods of unremitting warfare.

Defense, as a metaphor itself, implicates itself in and enfolds and questions metaphor. Metaphor of defense is greeted with meta-phor—that of map, of skin, of borderlands, of recesses. Surely there is a peculiar pleasure in tracing outlines, the mottled skin or shape that resists. Taking into account defensive measures means taking into account more elements of the poet's arsenal. And then, too, to try to locate a poem's defensive strategies means that we have to ask: What is being defended? What about the poem signals a certain vulnerability that needs defending?

At this point I want to return to Moore as the first of two poets we might at least briefly consider in this introductory exploration. To do so makes it possible to think about how a poet might defend her poem from within a poem (and in defending the poem, by im-plication, defend poetry as a form of defense). I have chosen Stevie Smith as a contrast to Moore because of the unusual extremity of the positions that are revealed when we consider these two poets together. Moore's outward power, we should note, is structured upon her nearly curatorial detailing of sensory matters that rely on acute observation of artifacts. In Smith we approach fact and knowledge in a very different matter; we do not "learn" about an outside natural world as it has been represented in photographs or other texts—not even remotely in the manner in which we learn of the "real" in Moore's poems.

In Moore's poems, knowledge and, in turn, authority appear to rest on the skin of the poem. Assembled and arranged, discrete phrases might as well be pinned to the poems, collected from tracts, sermons, and various manuals, selected as language speci-mens. In "Critics and Connoisseurs," as a fantasist of close observa-tion, Moore writes of the futility of "fastidiousness" without an adaptation to form and purpose. It is "unconscious fastidiousness" that she prefers, the task at hand dictating the means of action. Her poems in their fastidiousness seem made of small parts, odd spiny shells, brightly materialized as her crucial "armor," as Randall Jar-rell pointed out and as Moore herself would appear to allude to: "The staff, the bag, the feigned inconsequence / of manner, best bespeak that weapon, self-protectiveness."[24] A Moore poem may seem like one of her feathered creatures in which exact counts du-plicate an initial pattern, for Moore's are the imperatives of the ec-centric collector of facsimiles. Yet it appears that her inclusion in poems of prose phrases imported from various textual materials is not only one of the often-acknowledged innovations of her poetry but a means, a defense at work, in which thinking amounts in some measure to a collecting of defenses, as Jarrell suggests. In reviewing Moore's *Collected Poems*, Jarrell focuses on hardening properties in the poems, "a heavy defensive armament" in her creatures[25] and within the poems themselves: "a good deal of her poetry is specifically (and changingly) about armour, weapons, protection, places to hide; and she is not only conscious that this is so, but after a while writes poems about the fact that it is so."[26] He offers praise with stipulations against her reserve, but Jarrell is keen to show us that defensive reserve is part of the elemental nature of Moore's poems. The defensive crust of her poetry is made of precise learning and conveyed as if an instrument in poetic deportment and self-protection.

A Moore poem may seem like a remarkable mechanical invention, even a self-correcting device. But if her poems amounted to only ingenious displays of embellishments they would be arid and unlikely to provide enough pleasure for us. The tone of assertion would seem meek before the facts it celebrates. Instead, Moore's poetry is alive in its search for a precise attitude to put into effect. What animates the parts is not in the facts Moore accumulates but in the intervals between facts, as attitude notes are adjusted. What is crucial to her poems is a particular disingenuous tone of enthusiasm that develops, a tone that bears the impression of innocence and even near ignorance before the crucial multiplicity of her subject matters. That illusion of innocence may account for the strangely proprietary reception of her work and even of her person in some critical accounts. It is not the mastery over detail that makes her poems deeply memorable; it is the barely disguised sense of an amateur's avidity that is defended within the poems by a front line of fact and careful attention to the vantage points of materiality. That is, we read Moore in some measure for what falls between her details of observation: her sense that the poem's arrangements are precarious stays and fragile enough to merit protection. The front line of factual observations protects a delicate sensibility keyed to the very capacity to marvel.

If we turn to the British poet Stevie Smith, we see something of a quite different order but of equal interest. In Smith, as opposed to Moore, the surface language features of the poems convey innocence. Her poems are undeniably less given to polysyllabic vocabulary collecting and records of detailed sensual material than Moore's. Smith's attitudes tend to be related to grievance and mischief, attitudes that hardly strike us as authoritative initially. Yet despite Smith's linguistic markers of a seeming immaturity and guilelessness—her insistent nursery rhythms that Sylvia Plath, who counted Smith as an influence, would later parlay—and despite Smith's choice of limited diction, her poems ultimately give us an impression of authority as knowingly as do Moore's poems with their quills of minute distinctions. After all, what Smith's child speakers or childlike speakers know is in their terms incontrovertible and absolutely authoritative. They are the sages of the emotional playpen, keenly cognizant of cruelty and culpability, and unsentimental about their knowledge. The poems' defensive strength is invested in these speakers' clear-eyed acknowledgment of their situations and their appraisal of most adults as fools. In Smith, the child's voice creates defense. Such a voice cannot logically be argued with.

While we can say that Moore's poems have been assembled from varied textual sites, Smith's poems are congruent in their images and references. Even if their surface contexts may come from fairy tales and myths, the poems are surely not on anything like allusion-gathering expeditions. It is telling in this context that Moore's poems, unlike Smith's, are sometimes difficult to voice, requiring the most discriminating use of pitch and emphasis. Smith's poems, on the other hand, are almost compulsively sayable; they ask to be spoken aloud nearly in the way that nursery rhymes demand. Smith would tip the poems toward the pleasures of doggerel, as if doggerel were a defensive disguise covering the authority of grief. Her rhymes and sound effects march in close rank but there is something lurking in the poems, the final biting renunciation of the sentimentality that the poems veer toward but ultimately reject. Smith's innocence may be perceived then only as a surface feature. The "core" of the poems posits an authority while Smith defends the vulnerability of her personae through the certainty of their knowledge of ill treatment and their refusal to rationalize their plights. The seeming simplicity of language is in tension with the authority of acknowledged experience. The poems know their outcomes and their emotional truths and take some of their meaning from the illusion of innocence, in Smith's case the surface naiveté of language combined with an unaccomodationist perspective. While Moore is an authority on good behavior, Smith is an authority on bad behavior and particularly adults' compulsions to renege on their responsibilities. Smith's endings pull the poem up short and curdle its more welcoming dimensions. The conclusions of the poems depart often from the measured (sometimes cheerily and purposefully overmeasured and tightly rhymed) preceding stanzas. They interrupt, deflate, or cut off the original rhetorical trajectory of the poem. They are bracing refusals that interrupt earlier meanings. Their flat assertiveness brooks no competing interpretation.

Moore's and Smith's poems erect defenses then that are ultimately protective of conceptualizing states that are vulnerable; respectively, the autodidact's wonder that may seem gullible or overly enthusiastic; and a bitter knowledge that takes the child's side of an argument and as such militates against even responsible maturity. A strong poem may gain its power in part because of not only its authority but its awareness of ignorance and compulsion—the subject too immense for it and a sideways acknowledgment of mistakenness, a beloved that resists, a state of feeling that defies understanding. The labor of such poems is in some ways concerned with defenses, even defenses of their own labors.

In the following pages I focus on four poets, all of whom wrote in the contemporary period, two of whom are writing in the twenty-first century. (Lorine Niedecker, born in 1903, is generally considered a late-generation modernist, but the trajectory of her work, and certainly her reputation, melds into the contemporary period, and I have focused largely on her poems written after the Second World War.) My aim is not to defend poetry as an art but to point toward and consider defense as a mechanism in specific poems. The poetry that is discussed here establishes lines of defense, however permeable. Defense emerges as a resource, as even a tonal quality. In Niedecker we see enacted a defense of the endangered natural world and the endangered sensibility aligned with the natural; in Elizabeth Bishop an oblique defense of nonsense and the plurality of perspective; in Louise Glück a defense of ambition as the ideal militates against physical vulnerability and what may be made of "a diminished thing"; in Carson a defense of a kernel narrative of unrequited love as a failure of intimate and completed "contact."

In turning to Niedecker and Bishop, I discuss spatial defenses, the ways that these poets' casting of authority over space, that is, environment and locale, creates a protective defensive environment. Of course in the mobility of their lives, Niedecker and Bishop could hardly seem more opposed, what with Niedecker's resolute connection to Black Hawk Island in Wisconsin, as opposed to Bishop's early repetitive uprootings, her frequent travels and her long expatriation, experiences that are mapped in Bishop's poems by prominent and often heuristic references to the breadth of place. Despite these critical differences in mobility and lifestyle, or perhaps through them, both poets place their authority in spatial terms—laying out their physical surroundings and then showing the overwhelming and implicit dissolution of these environments. Within the rind of special authority over place, both poets project sensations of psychic vulnerability, through Niedecker's powerful experience of the fragility of the means of perception of materiality itself, and through Bishop's sense of being physically threatened, out of plumb in terms of her cultures, each of which seems at most tenuously adopted.

Whereas Niedecker and Bishop create a defensive order of authority through singular experiences with space, Glück and Carson are more apt to project conceptions of time in their defensive measures. Whereas Niedecker and Bishop write of where they live—with the perspective of outsider in Bishop or the permanent and (permanently misunderstood) resident in Niedecker—Glück and Carson write with their fullest energy as if traveling upon a vertical axis that penetrates time periods. Archetype and ancient myth resonate in the work of both; indeed one might argue that so obvious is this connection that much of their work is hardly conceivable without the poets' vigorous foraging through time. In Glück, other time periods serve almost as internalized ready-made forms. In Carson, on the other hand, myth and canonical art are to be explored etymologically and contextually but with an overlay of "distances"—a warping of one period over and against another, her scenic variables inquired into with the resources that she has developed as a classics scholar. Where Glück remains somewhat self-consciously wary of much scholarly endeavor and takes pains to discriminate between poetry and scholarship (although acknowledging a shared "passion" between them), one of Carson's contributions to contemporary poetry has been to expose and soften the boundaries between poetry and scholarship as she writes of obsessions that are mirrored and refracted over time. In Carson, chains of effects are to be reinterrogated without ultimate closure, as her redraftings and even obsessive repetitions of narratives suggest.

When we think of the personal voice and a poet who writes in a style that has been called "self-effacing" or "modest" or "austere" or "erudite"—capsule summaries that have been applied respectively to these poets—we assume that the primary voice of a poem may point to a subtly modulating sense of being, however provisional. Elisa New in *The Regenerate Lyric* writes that "poems that disbelieve themselves can renounce the one power they have: call it voice. . . . Whether the voice that utters the poem in fact owns itself, is individual, has some coherence outside the exigencies of the various systems that press on it—these are not easy questions to answer. . . . Poems cannot prove the existence of the integral self, but the lyric does not exist save where the existence of the speaking self is seriously entertained."[27] Writing in the 1990s, New limns the suspicion of the notion of the individual that dominated much discussion of poetry at the end of the twentieth century. The stubborn facts and seductions of discrete personality and sensibility as they interpenetrate the cultural do not go away—nor would all of us wish them to do so. As Susan Stewart argues in *Poetry and the Fate of the Senses*, "The task of aesthetic production and reception in general is to make visible, tangible, and audible the figures of persons."[28] Stewart's point seems true even for Niedecker, the most seemingly "anonymous" of the poets discussed here, as she has been described by Rachel Blau DuPlessis.[29] And yet surely, although Niedecker has been considered in terms of anonymity in her relative isolation and in her deployment of Mother Goose and other anonymous sources, as we look more closely at her work we recognize her commitments to place and class and the braidings of objectivist, surrealist, and folk practice as these constitute distinctive shapings that make both "the figure of her person" and the figure of the poem more recognizable.

For women, the issue of defensive measures may be especially complex because, as is the case for each of the poets discussed here, social constructs have been denigrating to their gender. For anyone to write poetry with sustained seriousness requires defenses against those voices that militate against a writer's particular beliefs about the nature of literary achievement. For women to write innovative poetry, in the periods when these women came of age as writers, required strong defenses, or at the minimum a strategic insensitivity to those voices that questioned (bizarre as such questions may seem now) the possibility of women's achievement in poetry. These four poets occupy the gender traditionally less expected to defend poetry successfully. As the following chapters will show, these poets' defenses are implicated in their resistance to expectations ascribed to both gender and genre.

Niedecker might seem the least defensive of these poets. She practiced what amounted to an etiquette of humility. Yet increasingly as we find ways to describe her poetry and its effects, we discover her means of drawing boundaries, of making a poetics that defines and defends its own practices. We see Niedecker writing a poetry of both materiality and immateriality. In her work we have another sort of partially grounded poetry—grounded certainly in locale, a deeply experienced physical world, but one in which images may bend and warp and in which the processes of materiality are made fluid. Like Moore, Niedecker inspires protectors and enthusiasm, and like Moore she writes a poetry that reflects the profound idiosyncrasies of its maker. She is a naturalist of her cyclical experience, yet it is her task as a writer to see the particular dissolve. Her own weak sightedness, her fears of going blind, and the deafness of her mother are figured in her poems. She has taken her sensory predicaments as one source for her writing. In Niedecker, the dissolution of the visual as figured in water imagery reflects a radically mobile poetic.

In Bishop the narrative voice inhabits fragile, papery worlds. Bishop's almost conversational ease, inviting, relishes the peculiar. The casual surfaces of her poems may be viewed in terms of a defensive rhetoric; what the poems protect is a scenario of displacement and the physical sensations attendant upon displacement, particularly the tenuous nature of construing tactile sensations. She invests in a poetics that is subtly aligned toward nonsense verse as it contests common sense.

Louise Glück writes increasingly of the erotics of distance. Distance is essentialized and ultimately sought after explicitly in her poems. The poems insist on their distance, psychological and spatial, as defense. Most often, Glück is a writer who resists good news.

An aggrieved sensibility underlies her poems, and their urgency depends on unmet needs, a vulnerability that cloaks itself in projections of self-knowledge. Her speakers dissect their own self-dissections, until we see a self as taken apart in the process of speaking and then tentatively reconstructed. In poems of later midcareer she risks a retreat to the stony immobility of her early poems, or a reversion to abstractions. In Glück the body responds to instinct, and it is instinctual response—and the particular fragilities of the body and the limits of perception—that she resists.

I close the chapters focusing on individual poets by looking at the works of Anne Carson, a Canadian poet who has made a study of the perception of psychological and physical distance as a prerequisite in erotic love. In Carson we have a kind of scholarship of extended or refracted quotation and reflection on texts; her poetics is structured by distances—the perceived distance between our contemporary situation and the events narrated in the ancient text and/or the canonical text—and by a secondary structuring in abasement, the story of love for an unworthy object. Carson works in part through an overlapping between often canonical allusions, alternate media, and a contemporary narrative of misspent, misplaced loves. An *ur*-narrative—usually of a woman losing herself to a man who seeks other lovers—is a study of the playing of distance, delaying and hesitating before the possibility of proximity as Carson ultimately circumvents or interrupts a narrative of fulfillment. Generic conventions are reversed and distorted as a means of defense, repelling an invasive reader. Where Glück writes of the impulse toward perfection, Carson writes out of an explicit and self-conscious impulse to limn the imperfect. She would make an eruptible poetry that defies ending, and she has risked critical charges of excess and of misplaced erudition in doing so.

Marjorie Perloff's question from more than a decade ago continues to apply: "given the particular options (and nonoptions) of writing at the turn of the twenty-first century, what significant role can poetic language play?"[30] These four poets provide different answers, but each offers us a way to consider poetic language as it creates experiences of defense as well as opportunities for putting forward assertions. We might turn to Charles Olson's argument here: "all the thots men are capable of can be entered on the back of a postage stamp. So, is it not the PLAY of a mind we are after, is not that that shows whether a mind is there at all?"[31] The play of the mind is various: assertion and retreat, offense and defense mark the contours of the poem. "A crooked road, a road in which the foot feels acutely the stones beneath it, a road that turns back on itself—this is the road of art," Viktor Shklovsky asserts.[32] That is not only the road of art; it is much of the very substance of art.

1

Humility Does Not Cancel Stubbornness: Defensive Positioning in Lorine Niedecker

A good deal of Lorine Niedecker's work has appeared posthumously, and certainly her reputation has developed posthumously, factors that have meant that as her poetry has been brought to greater public awareness it has met the narrative arc of resistance. Perhaps most well known is the early response of Donald Davie, who refers to some of Niedecker's poetry as "miniscule scraps of verse" and as "a litter of jottings."[1] One of the few severe critics to greet the resurgence of Niedecker's poetry, Davie cites against the poet what he detects as an aura of deprivation. He refers to her relatively small quantity of poems as they appear in *The Granite Pail* and *From This Condensery*, many of the poems cast in unfinished versions, as their author conducted a lifestyle that apparently kept her "in place." Literally and figuratively, her poetry concerns itself intimately with the landscape of her native Wisconsin and the language habits of its citizens, and reflects the conditions under which she earned a living: as a writer in the Federal Writer's Program, an assistant at a library, a copyreader, a landlord, and a cleaning woman. Davie views her experiences as a resident of Black Hawk Island as "desolatingly cramped" and culturally "impoverished,"[2] and judges her long friendship with Louis Zukofsky in terms of "tutelage."[3] When he turns his attention to Niedecker's defenders, his criticism is especially stern, for he accuses them of promulgating "a sort of hype that is mixed up with the crassest sort of secularized evangelism." Despite "the distortions of [Niedecker's] provincialism," and despite what he acknowledges measuredly as her aesthetic achievements, Davie argues that her critics have pulled "a specially impudent confidence trick,"[4] making hers a charity case of sorts—as if for the most part tautology and empty praise have greeted her work posthumously.

Certainly Niedecker emerges in some critical estimations as nearly egoless and subsumed under Louis Zukofsky's influence, as Penberthy in her painstaking scholarship has noted, defending Niedecker from being eclipsed by accounts that emphasize her alliance with Zukofsky to the detriment of her reputation. Niedecker and Zukofsky continued for forty years to maintain a friendly relationship largely conducted through correspondence. The friendship, however, may have created a posthumous burden, as Penberthy makes especially vivid: "Almost invariably, when the friendship is mentioned it is dismissed as tutelary—Niedecker as acolyte. From there she's viewed as only a step away from being an embarrassment, if not a positive obstacle, to the more serious business of true scholarship."[5] Niedecker, then, is a poet who has needed defending, and yet she would seem, in still-gathering biographical portraits, to have eschewed defense in her apparent humility before the willful Objectivism of Zukofsky and in her refusal to court the attention that some other poets in her generation more aggressively sought.[6]

If Davie has been censorious at points, other critics and the editors of anthologies (who tend to carve reputational niches most deeply) have been broadly enthusiastic, and it seems that in Niedecker we have a poet whose posthumous reputation is in the process of stabilizing. Yet until very recently, Niedecker's poetry led an island existence, nearly detached from the mainland of American poetry. "Every time she is mentioned, she must be reintroduced," as Rachel Blau DuPlessis has noted.[7] And yet the biographical details of Niedecker's life are reintroduced not only because readers are in the process of anchoring a poetics that resists "anchoring," but because of the very connections between Niedecker's material conditions and the practices implicit in her project. A consequence of her being "re-introduced" is that her poetry does not ultimately appear divorced from the material conditions from which it emerged: her class, gender, and regional alliances.

As we gain greater familiarity with the bulk of Niedecker's work—most recently appearing as *Collected Works* in 2002 under Penberthy's rigorous editing—we may begin to think of Niedecker as a poet not only in need of defense but one who practiced her own defensive measures, making a poetry that retains the contours of innovation into the twenty-first century through complex effects of dispersal and dissolution. The linguistic effects in her poems are related to her appreciation of her environment. Her poems are inflected by her acute consciousness of the very frailty of any means of sensory perception, and, in turn, by a triangulation of her aesthetic allegiances. Niedecker's poems, particularly those written after the Second World War, are conditioned by natural cycles through which she positions herself as a part and not simply as an observer, and by a deepening commitment to a poetics of location. Niedecker's poetry is immersed in Wisconsin's history and visual and auditory images, and that immersion is hardly extractable from her consciousness about her methods as they are drawn from what William Carlos Williams calls "local conditions." In a letter often quoted by her critics, Niedecker writes, "The Brontes had their moors, I have my marshes."[8] Her poems and letters reflect an exuberant delight in marshes, particularly in bird life: heron, whippoorwill, purple martin, wood thrush, and teal duck. She focuses on botanists and other historical figures and their concern with their natural environment. She discovers in her research of historical figures her own predilections. Nearly everyone she admires outright in her poetry is, if not another poet, at least an amateur naturalist.

Niedecker's letters to Zukofsky amount to an advocacy of place, reflecting what Richard Caddel refers to as her "objectivist environmentalist awareness."[9] Humans have adapted so well to an existence near water on the peninsula of Black Hawk Island that, like the animals she writes of, they too are made in its image. Her authority is in land identification and by extension class identification, in an ecology between the land/water's operations and her own and her neighbor's labors—in poetry in which the hard, clear edges of individual words are continually being modified, subject to and pressured by the pull of the contexts in which they are placed. Indeed her authority as a poet is rooted in a dimension of the kinetics of auditory and visual experience as these are aligned with linguistic experience. As Niedecker wrote to Gail Roub in 1967, "The basis is direct and clear—what has been seen or heard etc. . . .—but something gets in, overlays all that to make a state of consciousness." And later in the same letter she writes, "modern poetry and old poetry if it's good, proceeds not from one point to

the next linearly but in a circle. The *tone* of the thing. And aware-
ness of everything influencing everything."[10] That impression of
forward movement curving toward return animates much of her
work, particularly the late poems. Even in her most ideologically
fixed positions (her repeated opposition to consumerism and her
awareness of the way property rights interfere with public access
to lakes and rivers) her language is condensed toward new knowl-
edges rather than stabilized. When she works with a voice marked
by an occasional pose of naiveté, she invests the voice as being in
the midst of experience, implicated and inextricable from experi-
ence. Yet Niedecker's language is often so uncluttered, so "sheer,"
that it resists the aesthetic culture from which it emerged. She has
largely escaped a certain period styling as a consequence.

In part, Niedecker's complex form of condensing differentiates
her work from that of many of her contemporaries. While using
what seem like the simplest monosyllables, the simplest materials
and often—except in her use of nouns—the simplest vocabulary,
she has honed her technique toward dissolution. As Peter Quarter-
main notes, "one great distinction of Niedecker's poetry (her
chiefest is her sound) is precisely in this doubleness, this multiplic-
ity of effect, this simultaneous elaboration and *demolition*"(empha-
sis mine).[11] Niedecker enacts dissolution by presenting actual
flooding as a natural event and using floodlike figurations as a lin-
guistic effect. As DuPlessis says, "spending her life, she has chosen
poetry; the recurrent floods have chosen her."[12] And yet it could
also be said that repeatedly *she* "chose" flooding. Her lines in the
poems written after the 1950s, lightly freighted, are cast in what
Peter Nicholls calls a "minutely adjusted rhythmic 'wave.'"[13] The
actual floods she encounters nearly every spring teach that posses-
sions should be few, for possessions are easily, indeed regularly,
ruined by flooding. The flood suggests an absolute mutability.
What is tethered is tethered lightly. She reduces the distance be-
tween self and land and water to a poetics that reflects the proper-
ties of land and of water, especially the floods. Her images in some
of her most accomplished poems are often explicitly or implicitly
linked to flooding, to land overcome and transformed into silt. In
May 1963 she wrote to Cid Corman that it was "very unnatural"
that there was no flood that year.[14] Flooding, catastrophe, is "natu-
ral" as a physical event, and natural too for Niedecker is a certain

effect in her poems of both overwhelming barriers and retreating behind barriers.

Niedecker's later poems seem in perpetual motion. They are made of sliding stanzas, worked over to appear swayed by currents of meaning. She was particularly sensitive to phrasal compression. As a reader, quick to note perplexities in language, she used such tags as in "North Central" to investigate the human body as elemental:

> Far reach
> of sand
> A man
>
> bends to inspect
> a shell
> Himself
>
> part coral
> and mud
> clam[15]

This mobilelike poem is exemplary of much of her later method, as she renders meaning incomplete within each stanza. That is, each stanza creates a statement that initially makes sense on it own, but the sense it makes is modified in further stanzas. A man can metaphorically be a "Far reach / of sand." Here we see the interdependence of elements and meaning. We may ask, What object belongs to the principal actions? Is it the same far reach for sand, or man's far reach—or the far reach of both? The step-down lines signal a stepping down into syntax. Is it ultimately a man's far reach of sand that is being referred to? That is, a shifting movement without bearings? A similar effect occurs in the next stanza as the man must "bend to inspect / a shell / Himself."

Is this the shell of the self, or the self of the shell? Is this the self as protected, as made for defense? Is the man inspecting himself as well as the shell and, as such, questioning his own actions, how he must draw the eye and hand to the act of inspection? Syntactical interdependence renders the intricacy of meaning as hinged on a studied relationship between words. The short section concludes: "part coral / and mud / clam." Here, if we stop with the second step-down line, the self is a coral, an accumulation, a slow growth, and in turn the self is mud, instantly created. With the final one-word line we see that the human is part mud and part clam and also a mud clam, a shut-in creature that protects itself. The poem then posits an argument—that when humans look at nature they look at themselves—along with the suggestion that we are not separable from our environment and may bring the same inspection to ourselves as to our environment; our treatment of one reflects our treatment of the other. The man has had to "bend"; he must lower himself toward the earth and natural processes, but he is at essence the very creature whom he deigns to study.

Niedecker's poems are less collage-like than they seem to be precursors of something like the video clip with each image modifying expectations and propelling us forward with little ligature between images. Her lines, as we have seen, are pressured by subsequent movements that recast meaning. Her poems about water reflect not only on her sense of identity (effaced partially, in movement, paradoxically a subtraction of materiality) but on her poetics (effaced partially, a process of subtraction through not only extreme condensing but extremes of permeability). The work depends on syntactic interconnectedness, a line that moves forward and backward in which words must connect to one another in at least two directions, and in which words convey a kind of belonging that also acknowledges difference. To Cid Corman, Niedecker wrote in 1962, "For me the sentences lie in wait—all those prepositions and connectives—like an early spring flood."[16] While her letter suggests her "weakness" for the sentence, it also identifies how she works with an acute awareness of syntactic interdependence as much as with imagery. Her words seem hardly rooted or connected to a solid substratum. The stanzas perform as skeins of phrases, fluidly dependent on one another. Hers are poems of almost extreme motility; they live a life on the page in which they are subject to an intricate syntax.

An effect that Niedecker achieves and that is perhaps particularly difficult to describe or account for involves her ability to create the illusion of words that appear nearly afloat on the page, as if being printed above the material surface. Her poetry rays out, to make the page a surface upon which the poem shifts, an illusion achieved in part because of the labors we engage in as we read her poetry, labors that show meaning to be attenuated. Some of Niedecker's stylistic predilections may be accounted for by spatial arrangement in her poems, particularly those written after 1960. Each stanza may be arrayed like a ziggurat in the stepped-down order we are familiar with from some of William Carlos Williams's poems. White space draws us to the poem as marked visual creation. We tend to read white space as emptiness and silence—as absence and immateriality. Niedecker's eschewal of much punctuation reinforces a similar ungrounding of her poems as well. The snaps and stays of punctuation do not affix the poem to the page. The absence of punctuation reinforces the illusion of the poem set adrift and relatively unimpeded. Syntactic breaking points further reinforce the illusion of words buoyed above the surface of the page. Line breaks are often enjambed over stanzas, forcing the eye to drift from one stanza unit to another, evading a stopping point. Syntactic sense then is carried over, and we find ourselves carrying such sense past multiple lines and space markers. Nevertheless, such ferrying in terms of surface effects tends to be light work. At stanzaic breaks or line breaks we are not caught, generally, within a gnarl of abstractions or at a particularly complex conceptual marker. Lines tend to break on prepositions, on the class of words that are often invisible to us, suggesting relation and connection. It is worthwhile noting too that the words of most density and least familiarity—the semantically alien—tend to be nouns, often the names of plants, minerals, or other parts of an environment. As such, we see such nouns as temporarily stable elements. We accept their differences in the way we accept the name of a stranger.

As seemingly self-effacing as Niedecker's poems are, refusing to stop at points of identity or definition, it is the manner of their effacement that is striking. Niedecker's way of being seems to have been to stay out of the way, to register little overt resistance while quietly maintaining a certain and reliable defense. Nature becomes the scene of an encounter in which language-as-nature defends the poet:

> What bird would light
> in a moving tree
> the tree I carry
> for privacy?

> Down in the grass
> the question's inept;
> sora's eyes . . .
> stillness steps.
>
> (137)

The point here is that the tree is moving, and this volatility creates a defensive privacy, profferring both volition and motionlessness, a balance point in which a sensation of "stillness" arises (and yet is undermined by the kineticism of "steps"). Significantly, not only Niedecker's poems but her letters to Zukofsky suggest that she discovered herself in nature; she also kept her "privacy" within the natural, seeking privacy as ultimately a defensive stance, for she will not be absorbed into the social networks of other poets or into one poetic:

> We must pull
> the curtains—
> we haven't any
> leaves
>
> (242)

This slight, haiku-like poem says a number of things about poetry and privacy. The need for a defensive privacy is assumed, as is human vulnerability which requires that we retract from visibility. We may protect ourselves with the growth of natural form. And yet if nature creates the curtain of leaves, nature also drops the curtain. Only with late fall are curtains necessary, for nature in full summer (in its most burgeoning growing phase) is a kind of cover, a means to ensure privacy, blocking the windows and securing the poet's defenses as a part of nature.

By now many readers have seen Niedecker's poem of the granite pail often enough to fail to recognize how strange it is:

> Remember my little granite pail?
> The handle of it was blue.
> Think what's got away in my life—
> Was enough to carry me thru.
>
> (96)

The poem seems primitive and unrelievedly miniature. The pail is "little." The handle is "blue." The descriptives are simple and deliberately naïve. The opening question assumes a quaint familiarity with the reader. A rising inflection in the question bears a note we may associate with childhood. The poem's final two lines, however, work in steep contradiction to their predecessors. We aren't quietly questioned about our memory but instead are directed to take mental action over an eruption of meaning, to see actions in profound paradox. The pail is itself gone, after all. "[W]hat's got away"—presumably persons, experiences, even the language she has pared so relentlessly—has escaped as well. After the dash we have at least two readings to contend with: *Despite* losses, there "was enough"; or *because of* losses, there "was enough." In either case, the speaker herself is the one who has carried the pail initially and is carried again. What has been lost becomes a force; what gets away moves us in its wake. The poem is like a riddle where the agent who carries is herself carried, and where absence becomes presence rather than a prompt for nostalgia. The poem is not ultimately a conventional poem of renunciation where loss is sanctioned. Nor is it simply a statement of poetics as a discipline of condensing, or what John Ashbery called "this taking-out business." Rather, the poem is a defense of a poetics that inextricably implicates the poet in her own linguistic processes. If the pail is the mind, or the poem, or the poet (for the pail in context is not a static object by the time we arrive at the third line, but an object upon which the mind is invited to assign potentials) the poet is sustained and defended by her own actions, for the object becomes subject, the subject object. What the poet does with language "supports" her. What she takes away in her practice of condensing lines carries her. The poem amounts to a discrete defense of Niedecker's poetic experimentation. To "make it new" is to negotiate among choices, a process of keen discrimination. Patently, Niedecker's poems never let us forget a choice is being made deliberately with the finest calculation—and in a manner that allows eddies of reference to upset our sense of agency. Yet the lack of assertion of a highly visible and stable self-mythology in Niedecker's work does not, as such, mean that her poetry cannot carry the imprint of personality; a preference for privacy can be as much a marker of self-figuration as Marianne Moore's preference for a tricorner hat.

When Niedecker writes "I was born with poor eyes and a house," she casts a miniature biography that draws together essentials not only about her material conditions but about her aesthetic. Having inherited dismayingly frustrating and hardly remunerative responsibilities as a landlord, she is acutely conscious of living conditions—the difficulties posed by natural seasonal disasters as these affect a cottage. Her experiences of her material and natural conditions are rendered in visual terms often and, we should not forget, in the terms of a poet whose vision was poor and progressively weakened, and whose mother was deaf. As Penberthy notes, "Her work is distinguished by its attentive use of sound, a consequence perhaps of her poor eyesight and her experience of her mother's deafness, but also of her immersion in the rich soundscape of Black Hawk Island."[17] Penberthy also notes that Niedecker stopped working as a proofreader in 1950 because of her failing vision.[18] In December 1966 Niedecker reviews her past in a letter and the dire influence of "a noticeable failure in eyesight."[19] The dissolving of images—patterning that both braids and unbraids its figures—is connected to her actual lived relation to the senses which caused her grave daily concern, inflected in not only her poems' subjects but her practices. She takes upon herself an authority of observation that depends on an acknowledgment of the very fragility of sensory perception. An awareness of danger and threat is mixed with sensory anxiety in her poems, but so too is a particular focus on linguistic experience that would seem to be impressed upon her by her "poor eyes." Given that the very corruptibility and fragility of the senses were made all too real for this poet in her mother's deafness and in her own failing eyesight, Niedecker writes in especially complex ways about sense and sensing and how sensory phenomena impinge on our concepts. Bodily experience determines what a poet writes—whether a poet would attempt to escape bodily conditions or embed the poem with traces related to bodily conditions or form her practices to "carry / the sensing" (207).

We can think, surely, of Niedecker as a poet of advanced observation in a manner somewhat like Elizabeth Bishop, yet with critical differences. Bishop's poems invest in the powers of sight as sight plays upon materiality. As I will argue in the next chapter, in Bishop the visual is informed by complex processes of selection and differentiation of "the real"—on actual places and often actual

situations. Yet she allows to waver and split what otherwise might
be held as self-evident and self-consistent, admitting into the poem
perceptions aligned to nonsense verse. Niedecker's extreme habits
of condensation and her concentration on the actual elements of
her environment construct what we might think of as "the real" as
well, but with an ever greater attention to cycles of recurrence and
of material dissolution than do Bishop's poems. This comes partly
from their respective positions. Bishop, never entirely at home in
any culture, issues invitations in her poems to other non-natives to
appreciate and linger over an alien scene. Niedecker, on the other
hand, is almost obsessively at home, to the point where she traces
her lineage geologically. The drama of Niedecker's situation in na-
ture means that the perspectives in her poems cannot perform in
the same way as Bishop's. The major movements in Niedecker's
poems occur within the processes of nature, which the poems emu-
late as if they too were a natural force. Her poems move within
natural processes with the additional complication of a visual pat-
terning that dissolves the image in ways related to her experience
of the sense of sight.

We have in Niedecker, then, a nature writer of sorts who places
herself within the natural, and the natural within the self, in proc-
esses of identification—and with an increased pressure on natural
and linguistic processes of recurrent disruption. The "condensa-
tion" she writes of as integral to her method is not only a means
for compacting multiple words or an elimination of linguistic ex-
cess, but a combinatory force that casts words in perpetual move-
ment as modifying agents. Her poems do not occupy a single
niche; they fold in and away from perspectives, and they duplicate
sensory keenness and sensory loss. That is, they are inscribed with
patterns of recovery and of disappearance. The poems operate,
unmistakably, in terms of motion and reflectiveness. They crest
over a surface and cast up double images, reflections that suggest
the phantomlike qualities inherent in language as she came to per-
ceive it. Her lines do not convey a panicky stop but a step down
toward a not exactly solid earth. For all their awareness of objects,
the poems undo and dissolve and flood over the visual. Objects
then are in a relationship with the words that name them as solidity
is perpetually threatened and overcome. If Niedecker would sub-
mit, it would be to what her writing was increasingly making possi-
ble—a seamline between natural and linguistic processes. Objects

and processes "slide," in a method of condensing that allows us to experience not only compression of images but the shedding of images. Condensing, after all, is a form of subtraction. Niedecker was not only an antimaterialist, shoaling her rather small store of belongings, excoriating consumerist habits, but her poems actually merge on breaking down matter, on shaking any presumption to solidity in language, an effect that was perhaps conditioned by her own sensory experience. "No knick-knacks / between us" (1909) she writes, as if materialism obscures and prohibits intimacy. The poems subtract from their field; they serve defensively. Her wish to have her papers destroyed after her death is yet another unmistakable sign of her allegiance to conceptual dissolution. Her loyalty is to the mutability of language as instructed and corrected by natural processes.

Authority is a particularly complex issue in Niedecker, and yet it is in some ways the inescapable issue, for her authority as a poet is put into question repeatedly as readers question the reasons for her relative neglect. The terrain of her poems with their dissolving scenes, their linguistic play in which they seem to lift upward from the surface of the page—what strikes me as the most striking element of her poetic—is at odds with the conventional portrait of the poet as one whose work "stays" in the mind and inhabits a niche. We don't often think of our poets as humble. But humility does not cancel stubbornness. Her poetry relies in some measures on an authority of subtraction, subtraction of images of sensory acuity and subtraction of abstractions as her language is honed to reveal how much one word in relationship can do with others. Niedecker's complex positioning in regard to objectivism, surrealism, and folk poetry constitutes a negotiation in which she defends a poetics of such peculiarities, fortifying a triangulation among three seemingly distinct and hardly permeable aesthetic positions.

When it comes to poetry, argument is never enough. Poets may even be less compelled by argument than they are by recognitions and resemblances. Surely, as many readers have noted, Niedecker responded to Objectivism because she recognized the practices Louis Zukofsky described in the Objectivist issue of *Poetry* of February 1931. It seems likely that she first wrote to Zukofsky after seeing the Objectivist issue because she recognized something already within her capacity in a journal that contained poems by, among others, Kenneth Rexroth, Charles Reznikoff, Carl Rakosi, George Oppen, and Basil Bunting. Most prominent of the contributors is William Carlos Williams, for a poem ("The Botticellian Trees"), as the dedicatee of a poem by Richard Johns, and as a reference point in Zukofsky's essay "Program: Objectivists' 1931," in which Zukofsky focuses on "sincerity and objectification": "Writing occurs which is the detail, not mirage, of seeing, of thinking with the things as they exist, and of directing them along a line of melody. Shapes suggest themselves, and the mind senses and receives awareness."[20] The "object" would seem to be caught in a position that renders it wholly available: "Properly no verse should be called a poem if it does not convey the totality of perfect rest."[21] When we return to the heading of Zukofsky's essay we find a definition that takes into account the word *objective* as an optical term, a military term, and finally a poetic term: "Desire for what is objectively perfect, inextricably the direction of history and contemporary particulars."[22]

Already in 1931 Niedecker's level of accomplishment signals that she was responding to elements in Zukofsky's program that she recognized as both implicit and even explicit in her own work. In *The Objectivist Nexus* Rachel Blau DuPlessis and Peter Quartermain reflect on Objectivism's definition in a way that is related to Niedecker's practice: "the term 'Objectivist' has come to mean a non-symbolist, post-imagist poetics, characterized by a historical, realist, antimythological worldview, one in which 'the detail, not mirage' calls attention to the materiality of both the world and the word."[23] Before reading Zukofsky's essay Niedecker was already deeply invested in linguistic materiality, and some of her earliest poems rival found poems in their enthusiasm for disjunctive constructions and collated phrases. Yet for all of Objectivism's attractiveness, as Quartermain convincingly argues, surrealism will not be effaced from Niedecker's work despite Zukofsky's unmistakable repugnance toward it and Niedecker's deep affection for Zukofsky and sympathy for his projects. As DuPlessis and Quartermain argue, "Niedecker differs from the other Objectivists in that her work has a distinct, liberatory, pre-Objectivist phase of surreal writing, a phase on which she draws and with which she negotiates throughout her career."[24] It is through surrealism as practice and as potential that she manages to resist Objectivism's certainties, as

DuPlessis and Quartermain make clear: "Niedecker continues to take Objectivist poetics as meaning a resistance to association, to the 'streaming' of the mind at all levels, to any concentration on an emotional 'afterimage.'"[25] Penberthy goes so far as to argue convincingly that surrealism would "remain a steady influence throughout [Niedecker's] career."[26]

It is an intriguing exercise to read the poems in the Objectivist issue and the poems by Niedecker dated as being written shortly before or soon after this period. Niedecker's earliest poems attest to sound and word values and historical presence. As Nicholls points out, "it was precisely that sense of writing not as self-expression but as the articulation of the unconscious as something 'other' and uncanny which dominated Niedecker's experiments in the thirties."[27] Her poems of 1928 to 1936 reveal a sort of sensual and cerebral experiment that employs a self-conscious sense of theater. Her stage directions suggest her awareness of the poet as "playing" a part within language:

> . . . But who am I to observe
> myself? Dynamist for being out of dream?
> It's what comes of looking way back on the upper right
> shelf of the lower left cupboard; never be witty
> with any finality. From here, it takes so many stamps
> to post the most modern researches.

(32)

Note the self-consciousness of the poem, its tipping of the hat to dream mechanisms, and at the same time its keen awareness of economics. After all, it does cost money to send stamps. The calendar poems—lines written on a small calendar—on first glance might seem to betray their closeness to something almost like automatic writing and yet negotiate toward the highly discriminatory pleasures of placement. Such works suggests that surrealism's antipathy to boundaries was surely formative for her. And once capable of surrealist freedoms it seems unlikely that she would abandon its pleasures entirely and surrender to Objectivism without some sense of conflict. As Niedecker wrote in the 1930s to Mary Hoard, "Thank god for the Surrealist tendency running side by side with Objectivism and toward the monologue tongue."[28] Niedecker sought out Objectivism in part because of her attraction to representations and enactments of material conditions, but her triangulations between objectivism, surrealism, and folk monologue are not casual or accidental. Such approaches condition one another. As Penberthy argues, "it will take more than Objectivism to account for Niedecker's poetics of tact, deference, and elision."[29]

Niedecker's surrealism is abetted by Objectivism and her attachment to tactile ranges of experience—and by her sense of physicality which drew from unconscious ranges. Yet the spontaneity of surrealist practice alone was not congenial to her over the long term. She knew that she gained greater satisfaction through her exacting work method, her near compulsion to revise and to condense. Gilbert Sorrentino goes so far as to call the products of her labor "elegant, often wholly empty poems,"[30] a description that suggests the poems as being somehow containerlike, however elegant, and the focus of a near-spiritual discipline. Charles Altieri's description of Objectivism as "a discipline" may be especially resonant for Niedecker, if we think of Objectivism as a summons for generative practices. As Altieri argues, "Objectivism . . . is first of all a discipline of the poetic will and a critique of prophetic roles assumed by nineteenth-century poets."[31] What we have in Niedecker, for all her respect for Objectivism, is a resistance to the certainty to perceptual approach of some Objectivist strains of writing. She would avoid an ideal of "construction" of images and instead allow for perceptual shedding. Her poetry is not easily or entirely assimilated under a single rubric because it is a poetry of intervals. It puts into motion for itself the authority of resistance, a defense against encroachment. As DuPlessis claims, "The resistances Niedecker makes in her poetry involve her critical discomfort with gender norms, class assumptions, and American ideology as she lives out her intensive marginality to a dominant culture of materialism, bellicosity, bigness/bestness, and fame as it developed in the postwar period."[32] Such resistances are abetted by her stylistic resistances that develop through her attentive labors.

Niedecker, as we've seen, explicitly identified her influences as objectivist, surrealist, and "the folk monologue": "I conceive poetry as the folktales of the mind and us creating our own remembering."[33] In "Folk" she uses as her source the speech of her parents and neighbors, and applies the same alertness to regional dialect as she does to natural processes. Folk language, she recognizes, is her birthright, and one that no other poet can claim without having been raised in a culture still tethered to folk traditions. As a child of a deaf woman, she was perhaps inordinately attentive to the sounds of nature and of her neighbors. She was attracted to "unsophisticated" situations and speech for their hidden sophistication, their elaborate underlying logic. She works with the local particularity in showing how speech reflects environment among "the folk from who all poetry flows / and dreadfully much else" (142). The speech habits of locals intrigued her, and she rendered the most evocative of it without the sentimentality that mars some other poets' renderings of working-class speech.

And yet while Niedecker defends folk speech she also defends herself from folk—including family as folk. The busy, hard-working people whose voices emerge in her poems are in some respects her sternest judges. She must defend before them her poetry as actual labor: "No layoff / from this / condensery" (194). The poems are anxious to account for poetry as steady work. Time is spent, and Niedecker makes her desires ancestral and connected to the elemental. That she writes of cleaning, sweeping, upkeep, maintenance, that is, her labors in and out of the house—is suggestive; this is the work that is never done. It is the work of clearing that is aligned to the poetic practice of condensing, while nature continues with another sort of work that is never done. A well-known poem spoken in presumably her mother's voice echoes with what may been an accusation Niedecker had to defend herself from:

> I've wasted my whole life in water.
> My man's got nothing but leaky boats.
> My daughter, writer, sits and floats.
>
> (107)

Niedecker reflects on poetry as a sturdy trade, a "condensery," working toward great effects in a small space. She is asserting her poetic in a culture that would value one aesthetic direction more than another, whereas more clearly she would want to draw from the richness of competing aesthetics and be carried as a writer by her very alertness to the "local conditions" of regional language. "And don't be afraid / to pour wine over cabbage" (200), she writes, as if describing herself as a poet of sophistication who finds in what others consider common one of her readiest resources. To be a writer means then to apply oneself and "float," suspended between aesthetic strategies, never wholly submerged within one, but performing delicate acts of negotiation.

The traditions of surrealism and "folk" merge as traces in even so seemingly an Objectivist-inspired poem as "Popcorn-can cover," which retains the clear-eyed focus on the thing inherent in Objectivism, the make-do, extreme economy of a folk poetry, and an amiable suggestion of Niedecker's debt to surrealism in its hinting at the unexpected, the mouse that awaits the object. Clearly, the class tradition from which Niedecker emerged and in which she maintained allegiance and effectively did not entirely leave is a tradition of making do—of not throwing away but finding the most uses for one object. Objects and Objectivism are related to purpose in her poetry and thus to context as in "Popcorn-can cover":

> screwed to the wall
> over a hole
>   so the cold
> can't mouse in

(218)

Significantly this is like William Carlos Williams's "snapshot" technique—or like a still life. For all its seeming modesty, the poem is a remarkable piece in which the transformation of use and of context becomes a transformation of language. The repeated strong *o* sounds emphasize the force of the elements, even simple linguistic elements. Like the object upon which it focuses, the poem fulfills multiple purposes. The poem contains a condensed history: the popcorn as now consumed, the returning menace of natural elements (winter chill and vermin in a weak-walled house). In turn the poem is a model of her aesthetic: the favoring of extreme condensation and efficiency, a tone that makes us aware of threats to security, the transformation of nouns to verbs (that is, of objects into processes), the foregrounding of prepositions, and the presentation of an object's (or a word's) affixed quality (the "cover / screwed to the wall") undermined by natural processes, for even a metal plate cannot keep out cold forever. Nibbling at the image are the mice of destruction, as the final transformation of the noun *mouse* into a verb makes clear. Peter Nicholls writes about the poem, "In texts such as this, the pull of the writing is frequently *against* the image, with attention very deliberately focussed on the texture of the medium."[34] The poem tells us not only how Niedecker has employed the Objectivist focus on the object but how her experience of objects as a working-class woman who is also an artist is inflected in language beyond the object, for here the object has its own volatility. Something (and here we see traces of her surrealism) can "mouse" in. One object may mutate not only in terms of dual or triple use, but the language suggests nouns can leap into verbs, the inanimate to the animate (or the reverse), that the stays of meaning and use are contingent. We have her staples of folklore—the mouse in the house, the cold and the cover—but here too is a sense of imminent strangeness, the metamorphosis of language, that we attach to surrealism.

The tendency to defend, even more clearly, to justify, animates Niedecker's poems gathered as "For Paul." We might look at Niedecker's "Paul" poems as her most problematic compositions. Penberthy notes that Niedecker started "For Paul" in 1949, and tellingly, a year later Niedecker resigned from her proofreading work due to difficulties with her eyesight.[35] The poem sequences were often and somewhat torturously redrafted and re-vetted. As Penberthy points out, "Zukofsky's ambivalence was an important obstacle" to the poems' publication in book form.[36] Although addressed to the gifted son of Louis and Celia Zukofsky, the poems for Paul allow Niedecker to assert her continual vitality as a writer, to defend the validity of her perceptions, to position herself as a rhetorical mentor to a child, and to practice forms of folk talk.

The poems have their designs on us. They authorize Niedecker's aesthetic choices by displaying the range of styles which she allowed to be available to herself, and she turns with conviction to explaining her choices. She reveals both her rural background and her complicated recognition of the nature of the rural. Perhaps the pedagogical, didactic nature of her impulses during the period led her to believe her poems needed an addressee. In a sense she would duplicate Paul's practice as a musician: she too is practicing her scales and attempting to achieve another level of ambition even while disguising her ambition by focusing on a child reader. The privilege of Paul's gender, his parents' belief in him, his recognized and fostered talent: it is obvious to many readers that these could have been objects of envy for a writer even as generous as Niedecker. Instead of envy, she attempts an identification with Paul, a violin prodigy, asking that he participate in her life as she offers up her own experience. And yet when reading the poems in multiple versions, one senses the deeply conflicted nature of her project. According to Marjorie Perloff, through the poems Niedecker conceives a metaphorical child: "*Paul* becomes her own poetic child, a child Zukofsky may have fathered but which is, finally, wholly Niedecker's own."[37]

This may be wishful thinking, for Niedecker's form keeps shifting, never satisfied, never quite completed, and the poems betray anxiety about their own conceptions repeatedly, anxieties that were not entirely productive. What makes reading the poems at points difficult is what seems to be Niedecker's willful position, at the margins of an intact family, the outsider addressing occasions in a roundabout comment on her own conditions. Of course the Paul poems are self-consciously designed as experiments. They have the high failure rate of experiments and also the strength of experiments. If uneven, they are nevertheless fascinating, and they provide in some ways a moving enactment of a poet's endeavor to secure a justification of her choices.

The project undoubtedly raised a certain distress, not only because Niedecker wrote the poems to Zukofsky's son but because writing a poem to a child is a challenge in terms of tone. After all, Paul would have been a six-year-old at the time Niedecker began the series. How can Niedecker accommodate her own gift for nuance, her broad political and historical knowledge, to even the most gifted young child? Her complaint about her fading eyesight published in what Penberthy calls a "companion poem" to "For Paul"[38] might stand in for her own anxieties:

> Since I saw you last, Paul,
> my sight is weaker . . .
>
> I still see—
> it's the facts are thick—
> thru glass:
> a peace scare on Wall St.

                                                                (386)

Her ability to wedge war profiteering with her personal physical debilities animates the final line, above. But it is the sense of personal loss that strikes the more nuanced note; the final stanza, above, illustrates how difficult her tone is to establish. How, after all, do we tell a child so much bad news at once? What is a child to do with the weight of bodily and political corruption? Or the following?

> O Tannenbaum
> the children sing
> round and round
> one child sings out:
> atomic bomb
>
> (141)

A political poem written for young children in general would be difficult enough, but here we have a poem written to a specific child, a gifted child, deeply prized by his parents and, no doubt, deeply protected. How could Niedecker have not felt some sense of trespass—of invading the home of the most sensitive man she knew? And how can she figure the distance between the speaking self and the one spoken to, as herself a daughter whose worth cannot be as effectively displayed as a violin prodigy's can be? Her knowledge must be perceived knowledge, the knowledge of sensory experience, however weakened her sense of sight might be. What she tells Paul repeatedly concerns her own effort at stubbornly forging a position in terms of her poetry.

Addressing Paul unequivocally for his ability to make her want to write, she calls him "Generator boy" (151). But if he has been a generative force, he is also a knife: in fact, "he's been true to himself, a knife / behaved" (161). The image illuminates on several fronts. If we assume that by writing to Paul, Niedecker is constructing poetry that draws on inspiration from her own experiences, early and late, the image of the artist as knife is particularly resonant. The knife is a thing of utility and of violence. The image of "A knife / behaved" then insinuates the artist's own usefulness and also a violence inherent in art. A knife cuts—just as Niedecker cuts words. A knife pares; a knife eliminates excess. For Niedecker poetry is the art of precision, discipline, and choice. It is an art of behavior, of an almost extreme courtesy that should acknowledge the grief we may cause one another.

Whatever uneasiness individual poems may inspire, the Paul

poems convey those elements that Niedecker would most fiercely
defend. What she wants to teach Paul—and what is most effective
in the poems—is the lure of water in terms of her person and her
poetic, both "founded in water." Water is necessary and desired
beyond necessity: "by water they go for Helen" (396). The right to
go to water, a "right of way" is a right beyond property rights. (It
seems that one cannot write the natural poem over any course of
time without writing the political poem, for politics determines ac-
cess to the natural world and the survival of the natural world.)
Niedecker would repeatedly assign herself a portion of knowledge
and mark herself as part of a deeply meaningful world to which
others are compelled:

> Ask me rather what kind of people
>   —here they kick the book of poetry open—
> because you can't keep people from water
> they'll cut thru to it
> rut thru in the soft
> dig under and come up in the middle,
> by water they go for Helen
> in water seek their own image
>
>   (396)

"Paean to Place" refines and reinvests in an aesthetic of dissolu-
tion and proves successful because of its evasions and suggestive-
ness; it emulates its elements and, rather than attempt
prescription, it assumes agreement. It takes less care with its ad-
dressee than do the Paul poems—and surely Niedecker is liberated
in turn. Donald Davie, however harsh a critic, acknowledges
"Paean to Place" as "Niedecker's masterpiece."[39] Immediately Nie-
decker urges our understanding with two italicized lines set above
the poem's body: "And the place / was water." As such she puts
context into question. We do not consider water a place, after all.
The use of past tense also is not expected, as if water could partici-
pate in time itself. She conceives of origins as water, as mutable,
shifting, and powerful. And the act of *condensare* is the will to make
place, and yet to evade definitions too readily. The poem is a biog-
raphy of tenuous but finally enduring connections; the poem re-
flects on Niedecker's writing life, her willingness, indeed her
determination, to unite her poetry and her environment—and to

understand her relative poverty. The poem is an enactment of life with her family, revealing her sense of loyalty to them and to their particular passions and sorrows as each self-imagining overrides a syntactic stop:

> My mother and I
> born
> in swale and swamp and sworn
> to water
>
> (261)

The demolition of the bonds between mother and father are quickly traced as is the mother's solitariness exacerbated by deafness, and the father's own sacrifices in the family. Niedecker would immerse herself in cyclical destruction and remaking, imitating an anti-consumptionist aesthetic, for her poems do not gather so much as disperse material. Tellingly, the impetus behind "Paean to Place" is to "Throw *things* / to the flood." The self is variously a shore, a bird, a water lily. The speaker finds herself in a "floating life" (268). Water is a leveler; all people must submit to water—not only for purposes of life but in order to be seduced beyond static registers of being. As such, by focusing on a common human need, Niedecker attempts to restore or reclaim a social order of certain equalities and dependencies.

Mud is, significantly, "Water lily mud"—the elements are linguistically and physically changed by what inhabits them; language is understood only in context. We step over lines to confront propositional phrases often, and such a process reinforces our perception of delicate linkages in familial and linguistic relationships. The poem concludes with a cleansing, regenerative moment that ultimately suggests a larger scope:

> red Mars
>
> rising
> rides the sloughs and sluices
> of my mind
> with the persons
> on the edge
>
> (269)

The linguistic momentum, the overwhelming wave of time and language, ends with persons "on the edge," uniting mother and father and the poet at the margins of economic and aesthetic life. As many readers have noted, the image of margin dwellers unmistakably alludes as well to the other poets she counted herself among who were not placed centrally in the public culture of their time.

Despite its particulars, "Paean to Place" doesn't represent the accumulation of an absolute knowledge so much as widely spaced dispersions of knowledge points, and the whole of the poem is a kind of tensile net that has been cast to play against the margins of the page. Nevertheless, her reflections on material reality are here charged with expressions of emotion, suggesting that what she sees must be incorporated into her belief patterns. As Martha Nussbaum argues, "emotions are forms of judgment," presenting us with an "acknowledgment of neediness and lack of self-sufficiency."[40] As Nussbaum further argues, "emotions always involve thought of an object combined with thought of the object's salience or importance."[41] Niedecker's attitude toward the lived world she describes is inherent in the positioning and arrangement of objects as they are presented in a visual field that is "poor." Money worries, making do, getting by with limited sight and limited money and limited support do not cancel out another kind of making that is forthrightly emotional, however linguistically intricate.

Did Niedecker know her own power as a writer? A letter to Zukofsky from 1948 is suggestive: "I have a story, too, that unfolds & grows only in my dreams. I can't even remember it now. It never happens in waking life, only in dreams & while I'm adding to it in sleep I realize that I'm composing & think of myself as quite a genius."[42] Despite the gloss of self-effacement here, her letter reflects what appears to be her conviction that she must stubbornly persist in defending her power by her own methods (including the dream-logic of surrealism), creating a poetic that seems to carry its meaning lightly but inimitably. Or, as she would write, "how / often one takes his madness / into his own hands / and keeps it" (25). Niedecker defended her poetic by what might seem the least likely means of defense: ungrounding her poetics through images and syntax rendered in literalized fluid forms—and through an evasive etiquette that sought new effects in language by holding in suspension three aesthetic practices. She thought in terms of establishing a protective environment in which to practice. As she wrote to Morgan Gibson, she would develop a self-protective discipline of writing: "Getting up at 4:30 or 5:00 as I do when there is no possible chance of being disturbed and continuing till lunch time with my shell still around me."[43] By keeping in circulation within her own practices the primary poetics that she worked with, Objectivism, surrealism, and folk monologue (as they were inflected by her material conditions of class and gender and geography), she defends against her ultimate objectification. Her poetry achieves its effects through a particular fidelity to the physical materials of her experience as they are being abraded, dissolved, or put to other uses. In her scene of writing she sees herself as a worker engaged in a physical task, intent on a time-consuming labor, a worker who is compelled to continue with her labor that, while it eventually may seem fluidly spontaneous, is actually the result of the most considered and anxious effort. The writerly self for Niedecker always performs relatively close to the natural world, as she experiences it, behind "walls thin / as the back / of my writing tablet" (195).

2

Tilting at Sense: Defensive Nonsense in Elizabeth Bishop

Travel ensures multiple points of view. We might even say travel *inflicts* multiple points of view. Consider postcards as absence markers, recording our being out of our usual position, and reminding the recipient of being securely (and perhaps dully) in place while the sender notes her mobility and her pride in the fact. Elizabeth Bishop's poems of travel incite us to look at what is surely not before our eyes and not easily reached. Hers are notes not to the natives but to those who are at home, lodged in the common sense that her poems quietly tilt at, for one of the preoccupying dramas in Bishop's poetry concerns resistance, her barely accepted accommodations to reality as it has been defined for her, particularly—as many readers have noted—her absorption into even the most basic classificatory scheme, as a human being. The peculiarity of being a member of humanity, the insight animating her well-known "In the Waiting Room," figures in her poems throughout her career. Often she writes from the position of an onlooker folded temporarily into a scene before being deposited on yet another shore. The tourist or expatriate's eye view is a position from the margin that looks on what it sees as at least partly estranging; the central insight, the dominating moment is of only partial recognition. The tourist's condition is that of not being wholly accepted, or adopted, into a cultural order.

Unlike Lorine Niedecker, Bishop hardly seems to be a poet who needs defending (although Robert Lowell went to lengths to see that her gifts were defended and recognized in her lifetime). While her posthumous reputation has grown steadily, the threat of exhausting Bishop's work through familiarity does not seem a likely danger. Something in her work defends against too-ready assimilation. If Bishop inspires emulation in many poets and some of the warmest tones of praise from critics, it might be accounted for in some measure by the manner in which her complex effects of diction and syntax are put forward in service to a perceived vulnerability that merits our protection. The suggestion of a vulnerable oddity hovers in her work, even if accompanied by an admixture of insistent authorial distance. Like the prodigal of Bishop's poem of that name, the poet finds the notion of returning to human community after any absence to be difficult. To return is to acknowledge kinship and responsibility, and yet a form of self-estrangement. Bishop writes a quietly embattled poetry. As Joanne Feit Diehl claims, "Despite the disclaimers, qualifications, and play that mark these poems, Bishop's restraint has an ominous quality more suggestive than connection, a tenuous apprehension of a self moving through a world that is at once alien and mysterious."[1] It would be a mistake to ignore how much the tone of Bishop's poems owes to gestures of comfort performed to ward off panic. What's intriguing is a matter of recognizing what she finds comforting.

Gertrude Stein writes in "Composition as Explanation" (1926), "There is singularly nothing that makes a difference a difference in beginning and in the middle and in ending except that each generation has something different at which they are all looking."[2] If her generation was indeed looking in one direction, Bishop seems to have wanted to look in many directions: Wellfleet, Paris, Florida, Cape Breton, Santos, Nova Scotia, to name only some of the places directly referred to in the title matter of her poems. We might, however, take Stein's "explanation" as an initial point of pursuit when reading Elizabeth Bishop by asking, What does Bishop single out for visual scrutiny? We might even ask, What in language is Bishop looking at?

In this context it is useful to consider Elizabeth Bishop's drawings and paintings, for they allow another perspective from which to consider a poet praised so often for her attention to appearances. They give us another indication of what arrests her attention. Some of Bishop's most striking visual art presents temporary lodgings and worn-looking interiors. Furniture and fixtures impress us by their allusion to vacancy: empty chairs, lampshades that are crooked because no one has bothered to straighten them. The ceiling in "Chandelier" recalls us to her poem "Sleeping on the Ceiling,"[3] as the chandelier drags its shadow in Bishop's paint-ing, a shadow made to look like an ominous, appendage-laden crab. Rooms are often filled with, at best, make-do measures. One thinks of "Interior with Extension Chord" and how the chord, sta-pled to the wall and the ceiling, dominates the art work. What is normally obscured from view takes on a particular charm for Bishop, as she foregrounds power chords, phone and power lines, paneling, chord sashes, wood grain, brick work, fencing, and flag poles.

Bishop's paintings with their seemingly effortless and yet affec-tionate depictions cultivate an encounter with contingency. Some-one has rigged up these rooms, the chords and clasps and sashes. And yet, however casually the paintings appear to have been made, they provide us with a sense of the way her mind met the visual, for there is something attractively off-kilter about the paint-ings in their fixation on exposing conduits and contingencies. The effect is already evident in what William Benton regards as her "earliest known painting" with its doodlelike ivy blurred and smudged. The result is "an unrehearsed reality," as Benton writes, a description that could be applied to Bishop's poems as well for their illusion of casual construction—an effect that actually re-quired strenuous revision, unlike her paintings, as Benton makes clear: "They [her paintings] were the product and occupation of leisure, of fiddling around when more important work was out of the way or out of the question. She used poor materials, paper that traveled light and then disintegrated."[4]

Bishop is fond of what might be called the sensation of the untu-tored, not as unmediated, but as mediated heavily by detail, by perspective shifts that reject or resist well-established points of view. Even her seemingly simple studies in their focus on mount-ing details and the close grain of objects reveal a preference for delineating the out-of-plumb—and her stripes and highly con-trasting lines are most often askew.

Of course a painting is not a map of the mind, but a series of paintings may serve as an introduction to graphing a mind's pre-occupations. Like her paintings, Bishop's poems insist on more than the significance of contrasting visual details. They signal the importance of details that modify perception and give the illusion of our coming ever closer to an object or a scene and in doing so undergoing a series of mental adjustments that challenge our appreciation of aesthetic balance. Objects in her visual art may look as if tipping forward, ready to fall from the flat surface of the paper or canvas. Bishop's visual art, nevertheless, hardly seems to be about disorder as much as it is about the wavering of lines of energy that provisionally establish order. She creates flourishes on waiting space, tangles of ornament or lines bending against a realistic scene, as if to mark out the real as lineated. As Vernon Shetley suggests, Bishop is engaged in a "probing" critical enterprise "accomplished through her manipulation of tropes."[5] That is, she is an experimentalist of perspective. The beguiling nature of her poetry cannot cancel its capacity to investigate the most fundamental tropes regarding the way we make meaning by gaining our bearings, by pointing ourselves in a direction we consider suitable. Shetley in particular helps us to acknowledge how much of a repositioning effort Bishop puts readers through: her poems recount the difficulty of discerning a direction, and of carefully negotiating distances. This may account for the way scenes and people appear miniaturized in both her paintings and her poems. They are measured and positioned at a distance from the viewer or reader, marked by visual and linguistic space. Her consciousness of positionings is so acute that ultimately it suggests the opposite; the threatening potentials of being displaced meet the equally threatening potentials of being "in place." Neither alternative is engaged without caution.

The authority Bishop assumes resides in a visual foregrounding of the object or scene that allows the rhetorical field to expand by small increments, never more so than when Bishop invests in the whimsically nonsensical. Her descriptions, even the most inspired, announce their inadequacy. Thus the seemingly civil, understated tone of her work achieves its generative complication from the way in which that tone eventually undermines a vision of agreed-upon reality. Not only is the fish "let go" in Bishop's most anthologized poem, but an agreed-upon reality is let go. The poems work through an accretion of imagery, but accretion is not quite culmination.

Consider, for one instance, "Seascape," seemingly a poem of description but, beyond its descriptive devices, a poem about a means of perception. The lighthouse in the scene deems itself superior because it sees from the perspective of a single beam, a superficially rationalizing force. Nature serves the lighthouse as illuminated backdrop, celestially detailed: "it does look like heaven."[6] The poem is a relative of "The Unbeliever" in which a man who "sleeps on the top of a mast" (22) lives by his constricting nightmares. Like the lighthouse of "Seascape," the unbeliever imagines an outer hardness, a sea that demands that he freeze. His eyes closed, he is too fearful to investigate the world about him. Bishop takes her epigraph from Bunyan, but the scene is clearly of her own making in which a solitary figure inhabits a realm of reflections that he cannot see but can only intuit. The unbeliever suffers from willed blindness and precariousness. The lighthouse, in turn, is bounded by a startlingly limited point of view. We see the same typology—with differences—in "The Sandpiper," yet the bird's fixed gaze finally renders brilliance and beauty in its multiplicity, whereas more often the fixed point of view stifles in Bishop's poetry. What we see or refuse to see defines our security; seeing variously is a better defense than single mindedness.

In "The Map" we note immediately that Bishop's visuals are pointedly not designed to allow us to find our way in space or to calculate distances. Bishop's map casts before us an aesthetics of differences, where a surface slides beneath or over another surface, in a perennial "tugging." Physical instability is accompanied by linguistic instability. As Bishop's verbs suggest, this is a map where boundaries are eclipsed to be "read" as feeling-sensations. Names of towns "run out to sea" and designations for cities "cross the neighboring mountains" (3). She presents a textualizing of land, followed, at stanza's end, by what amounts to an undeniably domestic image: "These peninsulas take the water between thumb and finger / like women feeling for the smoothness of yard-goods." It is not an accident that the women are meticulous while "feeling for the smoothness" of fabric in "The Map." The domestic in Bishop is tactile, as is the aesthetic of domestication. The sense of touch is the protected sense in her poems, turning anxiously beneath the more prominent visual effects.

"First Death in Nova Scotia," with its emphatic place name at the title's point of emphasis, is another kind of mapping in which a child is expected to gain her bearings—although she must ultimately fail in doing so. The poem is a tactile-visual drama in which the visual becomes tactile through Bishop's rendering of the incongruities between the living and the dead. Written in the voice of an adult recalling the state of mind of a child, the poem encloses a child's attempts at understanding, and in turn her partial socialization into cultural orders. Beneath symbols of royalty and succession is the decaying body, as sealed off from the living as the beautiful and absurd loon "shot and stuffed" by the dead child's father (125). The spectacle creates an uncanniness. The willed effort by adults to aestheticize the moment with portraits and lilies is countered by the living child's avid attraction to the bright eyes of the loon and her desire to touch the loon's "breast," giving the poem its freakishly insinuating power.

The poem is quietly horrific as it unfolds its panels of mirrors. The living child is mirrored in another, nonliving child's presence. Death is duplicated furthermore in a preserved bird. Even mortuary procedures are hinted at in the stuffed loon; and rituals of monarchy and grief crumble before another ritual at the center of which is a very young corpse. The poem is about a kind of blockage, an inability to move—in that its symbols of ascension (the loon, even the royal family) are frozen. The snowdrift outside the door becomes the perceptual snowdrift summoned by the room's assembled articles. The most domesticated artifacts suggest the most eerie fate. Pointedly, the living mother has "laid out" the dead child, in a reversal of birth imagery, and despite the appalling scene, the living child's locus of desire centers on touch: the loon, whose "breast was deep and white, / cold and caressable" (125). What the child wants is the loon as an object to be touched and held. (Touch is implicated with the forbidden in Bishop's work and is the sense that is perhaps most anxiety producing.) The eyes are to be possessed and presumably pocketed, whereas both dead child and bird are preserved for the eye and not for touch. Even the coffin is "a little frosted cake"—something that stirs the child's desire, and the living child is physically raised above the dead child to present him with a lily of the valley. As in Frost's "Design," whiteness upon whiteness appalls.

In 1977, as part of a series of talks sponsored by the Academy of American Poets, Elizabeth Bishop discussed her influences. The expected figures that the poet and her critics have cited elsewhere, among them George Herbert, Gerard Manley Hopkins, and Marianne Moore, were summoned. Perhaps unexpected was Bishop's inclusion of the nineteenth-century poets Lewis Carroll and Edward Lear, with extended emphasis on Lear. If not strictly an influence, Bishop observed, Lear (1812–1888) was a poet whom she admired greatly, noting his technical value and characterizing "'How pleasant to know Mr Lear!'" as "practically a perfect poem in its way."[7] Bishop's recognition of Lear may point to her own peculiar relation to sense and nonsense. Bishop displays not only an affection for linguistic play but a repulsion from pure sense and rational agreement. To see through the "lens" of Lear may allow us not only to understand why Bishop would include him in a talk about her influences, but to discern the ways in which Lear's practices are duplicated at some levels in her own work, for in Bishop's terms a defense of poetry is, at times, a defense of nonsense, particularly the near-destructive element in nonsense—as it tweaks the cultural consensus of the real.

While Bishop, unlike Lear, does not engage in operations of pure nonsense, she assumes some of her power from an uncanny province aligned to nonsense. Denise Riley writes that "Poetry, you could say, is systematically 'mad language,' although not at all because of its authors' psychic tendencies, but merely because that half-latent unreason endemic to all ordinary language is professionally exploited by poetry. That—not something more ethereally glorious—is what poetry does, what it is."[8] Bishop's poems attest to a heightened connection to what Riley calls "half-latent unreason." Her poems, like Lear's, interrogate common sense; insist on changes in material scale and distance; displace psychic trauma on appearance and whimsy; and demonstrate an uneasy and yet wondering attitude to the physical body, particularly in terms of the sense of touch. What may be most compelling among the shared preoccupations of Lear and Bishop is their distrust of an agreed-upon reality as stable and continuous, presumably the province of mature consciousness. They offer what amounts to a defense of anxious peripheral states of consciousness.

We don't immediately say, how do we make sense of Bishop's work? Seemingly the work makes its sense for us. Initially Bishop's poetry applies what seems like a giant commonsense that is familiar to us, as if by replicating the quiet tone of one side of a polite conversation. Bishop's surface dynamics suggest near transparency. In her paratactic style the connectives would appear not to require a higher-order "processing" of materials. And yet on another level, we may recognize that her poems include defenses against sense. Their smooth surfaces admit moments of slippage and disarrangement. Underneath and within the syntax is her need for the out of kilter, an intelligence that releases what it has possessed because it has already in some ways overturned the object of pursuit. As Paul H. Fry writes, "I claim that poetry (literature, expressive communication), unlike other forms of discourse that exhaust themselves shaping or making sense of things, is that characteristic of utterance . . . which temporarily releases consciousness from its dependence on the signifying process."[9] The liberties we experience in Bishop's poems may be less due to a speaker's precise observations than to the way observation is shown to complicate our attempts at understanding agents and objects and any distinctions we try to make between them.

Susan Stewart, writing on nonsense, might have been alluding to "the beginning of nonsense" as a channel through which Bishop's poems pass. Stewart claims, "this is the beginning of nonsense: language lifted out of context, language turning on itself, language as infinite regression, language made hermetic, opaque in an envelope of language."[10] Nonsense is not practical, not fruitful, not serious—it is not productive in common ways; it sets up alternate rules; it is "childish," and wants us to see things "the other way around" as in Bishop's "Questions of Travel": "What childishness is it that while there's a breath of life / in our bodies, we are determined to rush / to see the sun the other way around?" (93). For Bishop, who wrote many letters but relatively few poems, and who excoriated herself for her slim production—and prided herself on her selectivity—nonsense produces anomalies that are generative and expressive of somatic and psychic urges.

Curiously, as if poets denied the benefits of secure childhoods might reclaim childhood in their poetry, both Lear and Bishop have struck many readers as childlike. Anne Stevenson, the first to write a critical book on Bishop, sets the tone. Bishop's sensibility is "distinctively childlike . . . with regard to human tragedy"[11] she writes, and Helen Vendler observes of Bishop that "when she is not actually representing herself as a child, she is, often, sounding like one."[12] Eavan Boland carries their observations further: "If she sees as a child and sounds like a child—and she often does—it is with the eyes and the voice of a violated child, which, in a spiritual sense, she was."[13] Violation may suggest the tone of Lear and Bishop: an attitude toward self, reader, and poem that reflects considerable unease over psychic intrusion and raises an attractively ornamented shield of language as defense against such intrusion. If "spiritually violated" as children, each poet in different proportions chooses to violate linguistic expectations. In turn, they share a fascination with inevitable processes of physical maturation and view the body from a self-consciously alien perspective, as if through the dynamics of observation the physical self could at least momentarily be defended from attack.

In terms that might also be applied to Bishop, Thomas Byrom argues of Lear that "his peculiar gift was to be able to express the undisclosed."[14] Interestingly, Byrom's observation may recall one of the more revealing formulations about Bishop: Helen Vendler's description of the poet's work as operating in "the continuing vibration . . . between two frequencies—the domestic and the strange."[15] The peculiar "strangeness" that surfaces when we recall the situation of Edward Lear, including his alien status as a frequent traveler and his sexual ambiguity, echoes in turn the vexed relationship to common sense and "the natural" that Bishop displays. Often both Bishop and Lear record something close to incomprehension before human organization and gendered relationships.

The body in both Bishop's and Lear's work is subject to endless false interpretations. In Lear's terms, physical transformations reflect an acute anxiety (men and women's noses, for one obvious instance, may grow "exceedingly large" or "luminous"), and yet disaster suddenly may be overturned. The Pobble mysteriously loses his toes but discovers " 'It's a fact the whole world knows, / That Pobbles are happier without their toes'."[16] Other characters are trapped—in a jar or box or bottle. Bodies may be senselessly battered, or parts of bodies may grow in perverse ways, and even heads may be lost in this dark comedy. As Stewart notes, "While all language assumes a possible society, while all language is *utopian*, all nonsense divides and rearranges any idea of society as coherent and integral. Nonsense threatens the disintegration of an infinite 'making conscious,' an infinite movement of undercutting the world all at once and over and over again. It refuses the uplifting note by which the world assumes a happy ending."[17] In Lear and in Bishop we see that the body may undergo the sort of division and rearrangement that Stewart refers to in terms of society.

In her earliest work, Bishop presents uncanny perspectives that bear unmistakable connections to whimsy and nonsense. We might note, for instance, the odd embodiment of the harlequin figure as city-country landscape in "From the Country to the City" (13); the upending of scale in "A Miracle for Breakfast" (18–19); the precarious position of the sleeper atop a ship's mast in "The Unbeliever" (22); and the fantastic defiance of gravity in "Sleeping on the Ceiling" (29). The latter poem conveys a reversal akin to Lear's sensibility through its upside-down foray into dreamlike logic:

> It is so peaceful on the ceiling!
> It is the Place de la Concorde.
> The little crystal chandelier
> is off, the fountain is in the dark.
> Not a soul is in the park.
>
> Below, where the wallpaper is peeling,
> the Jardin des Plantes has locked its gates.
> Those photographs are animals.
> The mighty flowers and foliage rustle;
> under the leaves the insects tunnel.

Two inverted realms coexist: the peaceful (and sophisticated) realm of the ceiling and, lower down, the violent (and archaic) arena beneath the wallpaper. At the poem's conclusion, we are left with the latter: a contest between an insect-gladiator and a battling miniaturized self, removed from common spatial constrictions. Although Bishop withdraws from some part of her fantasy (we cannot, after all, sleep on the ceiling), she nevertheless illustrates the ever-present seduction of nonsense: "But oh, that we could sleep up there."

In its companion poem, "Sleeping Standing Up," once again we enter a dreamlike reverie of inversion. Like one of Lear's nomadic creatures, Bishop's speaker sets out on a journey but fails to find a home despite, in reference to "Hansel and Gretel," a trail of "crumbs or pebbles." The purist is, indeed, sadly illusive, and no secure homecoming awaits: "How stupidly we steered / until the night was past / and never found out where the cottage was" (30). Likewise, "Insomnia" suggests her fascination with "that world inverted / where left is always right, / where the shadows are really the body." Amid reversals, another search for nurturance and affection is conducted, "where the heavens are shallow as the sea / is now deep, and you love me" (70). Through spatial inversion, one of the most frequently cited mechanisms of nonsense, Bishop would attempt to uncover new, vital relations, as in "Love Lies Sleeping" in which her speaker corrects herself and considers the "image of / the city" as it may be "inverted and distorted. No. I mean / distorted and revealed" (17). As Jeredith Merrin notes, Bishop's "trope of inversion is multivalent, a pattern that imposes its energy onto the organization of many sensations and experiences"[18] and is "linked to Bishop's sense of herself as sexually atypical."[19]

Similar early life circumstances may have influenced the two poets' attitudes toward language. For all practical purposes, they were parentless. Lear was the twentieth of twenty-one children, raised with little attention from his parents by his eldest sister Ann. When Bishop was eight months old her father died, and when she was five her mother, the victim of several breakdowns, was institutionalized for life. Bishop's upbringing was left to two sets of grandparents, and she was never to see her mother again. Marilyn May Lombardi isolates asthma and allergies as complicating factors in Bishop's development, as well as the car accident in which Bishop was involved in her youth and in which her friend the painter Margaret Miller was injured (Miller's arm would eventually be amputated). Lombardi suggests that these difficult experiences reflect the "tangled relations that existed in her life between psychosomatic illness and early maternal deprivation."[20] Lombardi sees Bishop's early experiences as predictive of later difficulties in relationship: "Whatever happiness Bishop found with other women grew on the hollow soil of a volcano—because, inevitably, she carried her childhood experience of love's instabilities and betrayals into the world of adult relationships."[21]

In her talk sponsored by the Academy of American Poets, Bishop quotes, " 'How pleasant to know Mr Lear!' " and ventures that Lear, while living in Italy, "wept rather a lot because he was extremely lonely and unhappy."[22] The ending of the poem may prove illuminating in this context:

> He weeps by the side of the ocean,
>   He weeps on the top of the hill;
> He purchases pancakes and lotion,
>   And chocolate shrimps from the mill.
>
> He reads, but he cannot speak, Spanish;
>   He cannot abide ginger-beer.—
> Ere the days of his pilgrimage vanish,—
>   'How pleasant to know Mr Lear!'[23]

This weeping and whimsical Lear attracts Bishop as he explores similar psychic territory and projects a self-deflating presence much like her own persona. In a letter to Bishop, Robert Lowell reminds her of what she had previously confided: "'When you write my epitaph, you must say I was the loneliest person who ever lived.'"[24] Like Lear, she confided her sorrows. Just as the tear is no longer attached to the loss of any specific object in Bishop, so too in Lear the tear becomes a diffuse marker of territory and an indication of an ever-present state of being that is in need of defense.

Like Edward Lear, Bishop charts a counterreality. In doing so she invents a gallery of more or less fanciful (and often isolated) characters to inhabit her counterreality. She echoes Lear's fantastic characters in her Man-Moth, the Gentleman of Shalott, the Burglar of Babylon, even the wildly whimsical Marianne Moore of "Invitation to Miss Moore," who is urged to fly over Brooklyn Bridge in a fashion that suggests one of Lear's ludicrous creations, "with a black capeful of butterfly wings and bon-mots, / with heaven knows how many angels all riding / on the broad black brim of [her] hat" (82). As Gilbert and Gubar claim, Bishop invests in "a fantasy, a daydreaming fairy tale about a literary fairy godmother in witch's clothing."[25]

As in Lear, Bishop's speakers are often barred from human warmth as they pursue imaginative freedom. A moment with Lear's "Cold are the crabs that crawl on yonder hill" may prove useful:

> Cold are the crabs that crawl on yonder hill.
> Colder the cucumbers that grow beneath
> And colder still the brazen chops that wreathe
> The tedious gloom of philosophic pills!
> For when the tardy film of nectar fills

> The ample bowls of demons and of men,
> There lurks the feeble mouse, the homely hen.
> And there the Porcupine with all her quills.[26]

What "lurks" is "the feeble," "the homely," and the "quilled" (or
resistant). The state of being excluded from dominant powers pre-
occupies Bishop as much as it does Lear. Lear's poem is surely a
send-up of poetry and perhaps, as many readers note, Tennyson-
ian gloom, its melancholy undercut by the comic specificity of its
creatures. Indeed, Lear's mock lugubriousness toward the "feeble
mouse" may have earned Bishop's special affection. Her own fee-
ble mouse occupies "The Hanging of the Mouse," a prose poem
from 1937 in which human customs and institutions are trans-
ferred to creatures recognizable from beast tales.

In its gruesome comedy, "The Hanging of the Mouse" (143–45)
proves to be one of the more anxious of Bishop's poems. It is a
miniature drama, drawing its texture from a linguistic finitude and
an impulse to miniaturize. As Stewart writes in *On Longing*, "Even
to speak of the miniature is to begin with imitation, with the
second-handedness and distance of the model."[27] Bishop's prose
poem links the rhetoric of the child's tale (and its fanciful and yet
obdurate resistance to agreed-upon reality) with the rhetoric of the
body and its disorderly resistance to coercion. We should note that
while social forces labor to govern bodies in "The Hanging of the
Mouse," the mouse's body, however ineffectually, contests order.
"At each corner [the mouse] fell slightly forward, and when he was
jerked in the right direction his feet became tangled together. The
beetles, however, without even looking at him, each time lifted him
quickly into the air for a second until his feet were untangled"
(143). While the subject body is inefficient, death in the form of
the executioner and his attendants is precise, clipped, and masked.
Between the official law and the doomed victim, a praying mantis
serves as religious sign: anxious, "a fit of nerves seemed to seize
him." Bishop places her subject in opposition to the authority of
totalizing institutions: the law and the church. At the same time,
she veers close to a world that, like Lear's, threatens to collapse
into meaninglessness and arbitrary signification.

Notably, details are conveyed with unsettling preciousness.
Bishop writes of the mouse to be executed: "The rope was tied ex-
quisitely behind one of his little round ears" (144). As he dies, the

mouse's "whiskers rowed hopelessly round and round in the air a few times and his feet flew up and curled into little balls like young fern plants" (144–45). The poem's partial subject is cruelty, drawn to our attention by an officious speaker who allows a narration of immediate perception to overwhelm any possibility of compassion.

How are we as readers to respond to "The Hanging of the Mouse?" We too are strangely situated, enjoying the sheer fictiveness of the execution scene and Bishop's oddly sweet descriptions as the mouse's suffering is transformed into spectacle. Tellingly, the mouse's final physical posture points to Bishop's frequent focus on the crowd's misperception of the outsider. "The mouse raised a hand and wiped his nose with it, and most of the crowd interpreted this gesture as a farewell wave and spoke of it for weeks afterwards" (144). A misreading occurs in which the crowd grants itself authority and meaning, making itself the victim's final reference. As Robert Pinsky observes of Bishop, "her great subject is the contest—or truce, or trade-agreement—between the single human soul on one side and, on the other side, the contingent world of artifacts and other people."[28] Here the individual subject is defeated utterly. Of course, the mouse's movement is only in reference to himself and to his own body; he must wipe his nose. It is the audience's will that falsely forces a communicative meaning upon his action.

A tone of near-desperate gaiety similar to Lear's may be heard in Bishop's work. In "Pink Dog" (190–91) a hairless female dog, afflicted with scabies, wanders the streets of Rio de Janeiro. The mock solution to the dog's predicament appears at odds with the genuine misery that serves as the poem's backdrop. If we argue for its empathy, the poem fails disastrously—unless we see the poem as self-portraiture and self-solution.

> Yes, idiots, paralytics, parasites
> go bobbing in the ebbing sewage, nights
> out in the suburbs, where there are no lights.
>
> If they do this to anyone who begs,
> drugged, drunk, or sober, with or without legs,
> what would they do to sick, four-leggèd dogs?
>
>   (190)

The dog, we are advised, must not be seen naked, for nakedness confuses, threatens, and arouses violence. That the dog, an "eye-

sore," is a mother with "teats" reflects a peculiar vulnerability. As
we will see with the poet's other creatures, physically threatened
and psychologically alien to their surroundings, their raw nerves
would overcome them unless they focused on some assumed or
imagined bodily enhancement as a defense from intrusion. As
Diehl notes, "The dog's raw, pink skin and her hanging teats re-
quire a defense that can be achieved only through the use of intelli-
gence operating as disguise."[29] For the pink dog, Bishop reserves
disguise as remedy, as public response to the dog's body would
otherwise doom the animal. But disguise means that nothing is to
be done; there is no alternate route other than a cover-up—and it
is her sense of the implacability of the body's demands and time's
requirements that makes Bishop align herself with the realm of
nonsense, for nonsense both reveals and metaphorically escapes
those contingencies. What is vulnerable and thus needs defense in
these poems is frequently the fleshly.

   The very maturation of the body and its assignment within gen-
dered categories may indeed seem a masquerade to Bishop. In
"Exchanging Hats" (200–201) Bishop suggests that costume both
protects and emancipates, exposing boundaries of habit and tradi-
tion. "Exchanging Hats" presents a nearly didactic take on the pos-
sibilities of experiencing beyond a presumably fixed structure,
even while the poem offers a "closed" form: envelope stanzas and
comic-audacious polysyllabic rhymes, as the genders trade hats for
a "slight transvestite twist": "Costume and custom are complex. /
The headgear of the other sex / inspires us to experiment" (200).
The insistent polysyllables intervene to arrest our attention:
"transvestite," "Anandrous, "perversities," "avernal." Even such
multisyllables can be taken as an ornate language costume of sorts.
If "costume and custom are complex," the line of difference be-
tween words is minimalized just as in the sixth stanza when we run
up against "what might a miter matter?" Here too the near dupli-
cations of sounds reinforce our experience of both similarity and
of minute difference, an echo chamber where differences are put
before us through slight modifications, mirrorings between custom
and costume, matter and miter, slippages between words and gen-
ders. As we see in "Pink Dog," a "fantasia" is called for. The cam-
ouflage of the fantastical proves defensive, just as fanciful language
resists the encroachments of common social orders in Bishop's
poetry. Significantly, Alison Rieke refers to "concealment" as a pri-

mary "motive" of nonsense writers.[30] Yet it is not hidden knowledge but an antiknowledge that seems at work in Bishop's poetry. Her closeness to nonsense is not a submersion in nonsense. She does not invest in some nonsense procedures to conceal knowledge. Instead she invests in sites for feeling and sensing that run contrary to narratives of expanded and self-consistent meaning. The nonsense elements in her poems, their shifts in scale, language play, reflections on whimsy and reversals, are pleasing to her as a poet and fulfill a defensive function. They deflect anxiety by refusing a certain portentousness, a certain self-seriousness that threatens to ossify identity.

In nonsense we fall back, to revel in sound and in upheavals of scale and positioning, and to experience the slippage between making and unmaking sense. What Bishop's poems protect is the knowledge of how contingent the powers of observation are (and yet how sensitive are the powers of touch as a means of perception). What is defended is a kind of upside-down logic we associate with a form of physical susceptibility. Nonsense is a perspective that refuses established orders, that leaves the world unsettled through fragments and contingencies. The power of nonsense is a power of defense—to defend against sense, to question sense and put forward a multiplicity of directions. It is an aesthetic built on sliding from exact alignment, of proffering the odd rather than the exact proportion.

In three connected prose poem monologues, "Rainy Season: Sub-Tropics," Bishop focuses on bodies as sites of defensive imagination. A giant toad, a crab, and a giant snail all take their bodies as their sources of ultimate defense. Rather than their surroundings or their fellows, these creatures' bodies preoccupy them, in particular their defensive capacities. Each projects a temperament and a primary sense: the toad (sight); the crab (touch); the snail (hearing). The toad exists through an enlarging and yet dangerously permeable perception; the crab through a nimble and yet superficial perception; the snail through a cautious yet escapist sensibility. Convincingly, John Ashbery has argued that the three prose poems are "actually brief, mordant essays on the nature of being." What Ashbery calls the "strange divided singleness of our experience," the sense of our being "part thing and part thought"[31] is suggested as each animal perceives itself, including parts of the self, as unavailable and objectified. Ashbery's insight further links Bishop's poetics to Lear's, for states of being in both poets are curiously divided, and the body is to be observed not only with self-consciousness but perhaps, at some level, fascinated horror.

"My eyes bulge and hurt," cries the great toad. Such eyes "see too much, above, below, and yet there is not much to see." This, we should note, is a real toad of the imagination: "Perhaps the droplets on my mottled hide are pretty, like dewdrops, silver on a moldering leaf? They chill me through and through." Although only able to imagine its beauty, the toad is convinced its body is "angelic." That the toad thinks so may strike us as ludicrous. Yet we must note both its capacity for self-apotheosis and self-defense. As a dark, ungainly figure ringing "a profound, angelic bell" (139), the toad both comforts and defends itself in a hostile realm.

The second figure in this triptych is pointedly alien to its surroundings. Indeed, "This is not my home" is the strayed crab's first remark. Like the other creatures in Bishop's triptych, the crab delights in self-praise, choosing to call itself "dapper and elegant." Embodying pride and subtle feeling, it invests in "the oblique, the indirect approach." The crab reveres only the qualities it possesses: "compression, lightness, and agility, all rare in this loose world." Its consciousness fastens upon surfaces. Aggressive and arrogant, it remarks, "I own a pool, all the little fish swim in it" (140).

Another creature altogether, the giant snail is "heavy, heavy, heavy." Like the mammoth toad, it too is frightened by its own size and develops a philosophy that reflects fear: "Withdrawal is always best." Although unable to see its shell, the snail derives faith from imagining its physical beauty: "Ah, but I know my shell is beautiful, and high, and glazed, and shining. I know it well, although I have not seen it. Its curled white lip is of the finest enamel. Inside, it is as smooth as silk, and I, I fill it to perfection. . . . I leave a lovely opalescent ribbon: I know this" (141). Passive, unambitious, and yet sensitive, the snail will lie throughout the night "like a sleeping ear" above a waterfall (142).

Each creature displays a defensive measure: the toad's cry, the crab's agility, the snail's ability to withdraw. The creatures form a triptych of defenses in sound, movement, and recessive secrecy. We are aware of a near-comic ventriloquism, Bishop's voice insisting on the creatures' circumstances as an exercise in language and tone, even ultimately a study in personality type and in how far we are from an adequate understanding of our own physical being. The consciousness of each creature is cast in the language of protection and limitation.

Bishop's subtropical creatures live in fluid, the element (particularly in the form of the tear) that proves a sign of pain and bafflement, and conversely, regeneration, in this poetry. Helen Vendler examines the tear as physical sign in "Rainy Season: Sub-Tropics" and elsewhere in Bishop's body of work: "The tear—round, purse, tensely concentric, a small reflecting globe, a secretion of pain—is Bishop's most justifiably famous definition of a poem."[32] To return briefly to "The Hanging of the Mouse," a false tear in that poem suggests that the tear itself is variously determined for Bishop. During the "touching" execution, a cat's tears are irritants to her kitten: "They rolled down on to the child's back and he began to squirm and shriek, so that the mother thought that the sight of the hanging had perhaps been too much for him, but an excellent moral lesson, nevertheless" (145). The prose poem ends with a tear as conclusion to a Victorian lesson. In Bishop, the tear is a lens, fulfilling so many purposes that it is pervasive, an intimate secretion that evades simple meaning. Often, for instance, the tear is a distillate of the past. In "Chemin de Fer" a pond must "lie like an old tear / holding onto its injuries / lucidly year after year" (8). The tear is her inverted creature the Man-Moth's "only possession" (15). In "Sestina" (123) with its repetition of tears as one of the form's terminal words, a child's sense of time is reflected through tears. In "Song for the Rainy Season," a companion poem, broadly, to "Rainy Season: Sub-Tropics," the rain / drops/ tears form a protective barrier (101–2), muting outer turbulence and creating a lover's private sanctuary.

Why are these poems such piquant portrayals, divested of dimensionality, the physical suffering pointed to here made at key moments into something like cartoonery? In some ways, the poems that we have discussed as linked to Lear are Bishop's "problem" poems. Their circumstances—of public execution, obscure threats, disease, estrangement—are likely to invite our sympathies, but the stylistic treatment of her vehicles (a timorous mouse, tropical creatures, a dog afflicted with scabies) deflect attention to surface craft. Her speaker's management of tone in "The Hanging of the Mouse" and "Pink Dog," and in turn the mordant self-consciousness of her tropical animals, further rupture our responses.

The fact that Bishop plied Moore with visits to the circus to see animals there seems in this context particularly telling. Already in her second letter to Moore (April 4, 1934), Bishop issues a circus invitation to her older friend.[33] Bishop's letter is among the most delicately noninvasive invitations one could imagine. It comes as no surprise that Moore accepted. It seems likely that the circus animals presented more than simple amusement for both poets. Animals in a circus are put into a human context, their alien qualities brought into magnification. And yet because such animals are trained to attempt human actions, we are able to contemplate our own sense of coercion as a double estrangement, as instinct is defeated or retrained or manipulated for cultural ends. It is not accidental that the animals in Bishop's poem are most often drawn as humanlike. In one way or another most of her figures of animals are composites. Like the Man-Moth, a character inspired by a printer's error, they are born of slips of language and characterization, of imagining human intellect in a nonhuman form. Nearly all her animals (with the partial exception of the moose in the poem of that name) are anthropomorphized and are given defensive mechanisms that we associate with humans. Their instincts have been tampered with; they fascinate in part because they mirror us.

"The Man-Moth" is striking for its cartoonlike irreality. Yet Bishop has created a representation of a pained but dogged isolation in the figure of the shy and vulnerable Man-Moth, ever aspiring in his black and white hyperreality. The Man-Moth emerges as insectlike and manlike, a creature reminiscent of Gregor Samsa as cockroach, here redeemed and yet unmistakably harried. As David Kalstone observes, for the Man-Moth "the claims of the world come almost as a physical shock."[34] Just as this creature cannot tell temperature, he cannot "tell the rate at which he travels" backward. As we have noted, the Man-Moth unites the human and the animal explicitly—although the tropes of Bishop's work have posed animals as mirrors to humans. Like the child of "First Death in Nova Scotia" the Man-Moth fumbles at explanations that ultimately reduce complexity in favor of parallels to his limiting perception. His aim, however, is enormous: to move through the actual, to "push his small head through that round clean open-ing." That is, he would be born out of nature. It is an old human desire, despite the parenthesis that Bishop quickly applies: "(Man, standing below him, has no such illusions)" (14).

This creature, hands most often in back pockets, given to repetition, afraid of what he might see, rewards attention. The Man-Moth is a figuration of psychic needs, pointedly a creature aligned to nonsense, for he is born of an error in language. His "tear" is what "he'll hand over / cool as from underground springs and pure enough to drink" (15). It is what he has made in his urban environment, in his fear and susceptibility. This action of guarding a secretion marks the Man-Moth as defensive, prone to see himself "the wrong way," his tear the undiluted product of a fantastical life that requires extraordinary vigilance.

"The Man-Moth" carries the mark of whole-scale, willed invention. It doesn't, for instance, create the illusion of spontaneity or of natural movement. After the short first line of each stanza, the poem runs in long blocks, with frequent whole or partial stops within lines. The poem ends with an image of the eye itself as the night in which the creature most fully lives; the eye of Bishop's description, with the tear that is produced under distress and immediately hidden. It is the act of another's looking that means the tear will be relinquished. For this, the observer's patience is required, for the Man-Moth defends himself and recognizes himself as a secret agent of sorts—an agent of secrets.

In Bishop to set out, to leave a place, instills excitement. To return reflects failure of sorts, a deflation of possibility. Such restlessness marks most of her poetry, especially as she defends against the stable family order as it may duplicate confounding and confining likenesses. "The Prodigal" (71), one of Elizabeth Bishop's best known poems, enacts the sensory claustrophobia of a man who cannot, even in changing his allegiance temporarily to another species, fall out of culture. The prodigal is a composite in a subtle sense; animal and human orders interpenetrate once again. The poem opens with the prodigal among swine, gradually recognizing and giving in partially, never completely, to the animal realm. As a swineherd living among pigs, the prodigal has immersed himself, bizarrely, in more-of-the-same of what he has sought to escape. The intense psychic intrusiveness of family life as it is seen by

Bishop is made into a form of "piggishness" in the prodigal's mind. The pigs, "self-righteous," each with a "cheerful stare," take on human qualities, even down to a literalized rather than a metaphorical destruction of their offspring. The very air the prodigal breathes is inundated with animal waste and, in turn, in its bleakest terms the family is implicated as a scene of waste, where the "self-righteous" and "the cheerful" cannibalize the young. The second stanza with its biblical reference casts images seemingly like something out of a child's illustrated bible—until the poem implicates the prodigal's sexuality, as if sexuality and compelled human need must force his return home: "his shuddering insights, beyond his control, / touching him." It is the prodigal's instinctive sexuality that draws him back to the human world; his tactile desire returns him to the human family. But it is a quarrel between conceptions of mind and body that requires him to take his time before returning, for it is the mind that revolts against the flesh in this poem. The poem amounts to a study in repulsion, its image of "glass-smooth dung" suggesting further that the barn is a *mirror* of waste and decay. The final stroke that annihilates the poem's mounting irony takes place with a characteristic turn in Bishop: "But it took him a long time / finally to make up his mind to go home."

The prodigal's return is not a celebratory one, but a grudging one, and the close rhymes earlier in the poem further tap in the boards of compressed linguistic form, reinforcing intimations of familial claustrophobia (emphasized further by the assonance of *control* and *home*). We want the prodigal out of the barn, out of waste, beyond "a slimy board" as he halts with a bucket, but we are not comfortable with his return, for we know through the poem's agency how thin the membrane is between the human and the animal under human dominion, and how deeply the prodigal wishes to escape not only the physical dominion of others but their conceptual dominion as well.

"The Prodigal" is, in some measure, a poem about the failure of maturation, about an inability to construct another perspective beyond one's first home. The poem makes no mistake about the difficulty of human community, even when bestial conditions are the alternative. It is a poem that assumes psychological distance as a defensive measure but questions if we can ultimately defend ourselves against the metaphors through which we have learned to "experience our experience." Such learning seemingly can hardly be unlearned, and perhaps never completely.

Through the body's counterresponse to coercion in her poems, Bishop contests sense in a way that we may once again link to childhood. Children in her poetry are dramatically isolated and preoccupied by physical changes and maturation. Their status as at least partly outside the system of mature acculturation makes it more likely for them to wonder at the "natural" order of things. In one of her most discussed poems, "In the Waiting Room," a child finds bodies to be gruesome and fragmented. As many readers note, the child's fear of consciousness of self and group (and her relationship to both) is at least partly founded upon her distress over ascribed gender. In the dentist's waiting room, her perception of the African women in the *National Geographic* whose "awful hanging breasts" alarm her, reflects her own intimations of future maturity and her view of the body itself as a painfully disruptive force. Similarly, in "Crusoe in England" we may note the incongruously quiet understatement in Crusoe's depiction of Friday: "Friday was nice" (165) and later "—Pretty to watch; he had a pretty body" (166). The body emerges as an object for fascinated observation. Yet although Bishop's vision, like Lear's, has often been characterized as childlike, finally her vision does not reflect truly childlike concerns. More than a child's vision, I would suggest, Bishop's is an adult's baffled incomprehension at accepted classifications and orders in culture. If not wholly investing in the nonsense of Lear, as I have suggested, Bishop finds in the nineteenth-century nonsense poet another isolated sensibility assuming language as elaborate defense against psychic and critical appropriation.

In Bishop's poems we are either unsheltered, unhoused, or pinned in claustrophobia. Like the speaker in the widely anthologized "The Fish" (42) we are most often rocking in a "rented" boat—poised on cultural constructs that at some level militate against us. Indeed "The Fish" may be particularly important, for in that poem the fish is a caught creature—perhaps a figure for the poem—imposed between elements, half in and half out of water and between categories of being and nonbeing. When considered alongside Lear's poetic, it seems that Bishop certainly felt like letting the poem go. It is especially telling that Bishop would "let the fish go" in her most anthologized poem. Bishop referred to the

poem as "that damned 'Fish'" in a letter to Robert Lowell and
threatened to transform it into a sonnet.[35] As Doreski points out,
"Bishop's boredom and dissatisfaction with the poem suggests a
fear that the poem settles into sentiment instead of expanding into
true wisdom."[36] Repeatedly the fish is anthropomorphized in the
poem, unmistakably as if it were a war hero of sorts, and finally
the creature's multiple positioning confounds categories as an ele-
ment of nature or an element of art (for repeatedly it is defined in
terms of human artifice). Ultimately this fish doesn't fight for its
freedom but creates a mystery so compelling that the rainbow of
bilge around the fisherwoman is not only emitted by pollutants
but from the sight of the body before her. In Bishop's encounter,
the fish's record of successful defenses prompts the fisherwoman
to surrender the fish—and the poem. Both fish and poem are
packed in images that refute more common schemes of recogni-
tion. We meet images refracted through reflections of one an-
other. To see is to catch bright flashes, glittering scales like those
of "At the Fishhouses." We are dislocated because we are held in
these bright presentations. Ultimately the fish may seem, as it is
surrendered, to be the poem itself, which in the reading experi-
ence must elude the reader, just as the fish, simultaneously, must
be "let go."

Of course the ending of "The Fish" is so familiar to most readers
that it is hard now to imagine any other ending for it. Certainly it
hardly seems as if the fish would be hauled into the rowboat to ap-
pear later at table. And yet what we may take away from "The
Fish" is how insistently Bishop casts her creature as defensive.
After all, the fish's gills and lips are dangerous, each "weaponlike";
the fish is overhung with war medals. Yet it does not attack; it de-
fends. It has escaped being possessed. Like Bishop's poem in
which it is suspended for inspection, the fish may be taken up for
close observation, with care—and there we'll see her tropes of the
shallow surface as well as the self-possession of her poems, their
distancing perspectives, as these defend against readerly posses-
sion. At this point we might recall that Bishop writes in "Argu-
ment":

> Distance: Remember all that land
> beneath the plane;
> that coastline

of dim beaches deep in sand
stretching indistinguishably
all the way,
all the way to where my reasons end?

(81)

The manipulation of distance is a manipulation of sense in her poems, sense as related to questions of intimacy and propriety, and self-exposure.

3
Erotic Distances: Defensive Elevations in Louise Glück

Louise Glück's poems are not, nor were they designed to be, an achievement in what we would normally think of as human intimacy. We do not turn to Glück's poetry to witness intimacy between characters or between author and readers, but to experience a voice's stubborn territoriality, its imagining of and defense of its own value. The poems seem to work as if they were posthumously assembled at times, accounting for the meaning of a persona's earlier mistakes and yet suggesting that such mistakes may have been inevitable. What is meaning or intention compared to outcomes that are fated and inexorable? For all their control, their unrelenting movement where one proposition gives the illusion of inevitably leading to the next, Glück's poems rely on their suspicion of the seemingly natural and an almost resentful acknowledgment of human needs. The poems most often focus on recognition—recognition of patterns of behavior, of attraction and repulsion. They name the self's wants in terms of symptoms. But recognition is not intimacy. "My preference, from the beginning, has been the poetry that requests or craves a listener,"[1] Glück has written. Yet with their steely self-suspicion, their stern accusations, her poems have designs on us that are beyond intimacy.

For all its impassioned subject matter, Glück's poetry conveys a certain emotional remoteness from readers. Glück is defensive, opposing any imposition, preferring to believe in the written word as a call or invitation, an unwilled summons: "As a reader, consequently as a writer, I am partial to most forms of voluntary silence. I love what is implicit or present in outline, that which summons (as opposed to imposes) thought."[2] This tendency appears rooted in temperament, in her earliest formations of identity as she has described a common defense strategy of her adolescence. "What I could say was *no*: the way I saw to separate myself, to establish a self with clear boundaries, was to oppose myself to the declared desire of others, utilizing their wills to give shape to my own."[3] Her poems, and even her essays, make their case in part by distancing—distancing the poet from mundane experience (for the ordinary event is often transmuted to a higher power in Glück), insisting on an unwilled and uncontrollable source of inspiration, and projecting voices that are privy to an emotional context presented in only the barest outline. There has long been a chilly sense of elevation in the poems, as if the speaker were self-divided, one half of her the suffering woman caught in language, the other half the analyst of such language. The way Sylvia Plath harnessed anger for the lyric poem, Glück harnessed repulsion. She is not a poet of the democratic impulse, not a welcoming poet, but solitary in certain ways, writing a poetry of unflinching warnings. But as Nick Halpern asks, "what if a disgusted turning away were a *way* of being human, a way of living an everyday life?"[4]

The visual detail of a Bishop poem has almost no counterpart in Glück's entire body of work. In turn, the passionate denunciations of sexual desire and instinct in Glück have no counterpart in Bishop's work, although Bishop's poetry is marked by her unease about physical desire. With the "awful cheerfulness," the tonal qualifications that Bishop applies, and an attitude that ruefully often stops short at direct complaints of sorrow, Bishop would seem a poet vastly different from Louise Glück. Even a poem like Bishop's "One Art," with its clear acknowledgment of personal losses, insists on a form of stoicism, whereas Glück focuses on the utter lack of remedies and the stubborn implacability of what appears to be fate. The energy of Bishop's and Glück's poems is disported and directed in opposite ways. Bishop's poems move outward to her vistas and rooms; Glück's move inward toward psychic interrogation. Where Bishop casts her authority through her powers as an observer of physical reality, Glück casts hers as an observer of psychic reality. We might almost think of Bishop and Glück as profound opposites—except that both poets in very different ways contest accepted social orders and find the means to locate their defensive anxieties in their poetry.

The ordinary is most often suddenly strange in Glück's work—gingerly touched, glancingly touched. In *Meadowlands* (1996) the inclusion of references to dailiness ("the charged trivia of daily life") is heralded as a mark of distinction on the book jacket, as if the common presented without being sacralized were a difficult undoing of Glück's poetic, as perhaps it is. Yet when we read the poems that follow *Meadowlands* it becomes evident that however much Glück chooses to experiment with style and approach in each new collection, she is finally a poet who draws toward idealized projections. Even if she immerses herself in the ordinary it is to point toward the extraordinary. For all its focus on dailiness and common transitory moments, in *Meadowlands* it's not enough to get a divorce—one must bring Odysseus into the picture. But her tendency to enlarge and idealize, combined with a self-interrogation of motives, has made Glück's a voice of sustained power and complexity.

In repetitions of imagery and grievance, Glück's poetry seems unmistakably autobiographical. The primary personae have far too much in common not to be identified as a continuum of one personality meeting the vicissitudes of life from book to book. A biographical focus, no matter how stringently applied, will draw its detractors, some charging solipsism. Brian Henry refers to the "continued fetishization of [Glück's] life and her self," arguing that she "mines her private life in a way both exhibitionistic and narcissistic."[5] Glück's poems are, in some senses, as Henry suggests, "monumentalizing." The individual life achieves a momentous pattern linked to the mysteries of identity and purpose, principally through an atmosphere of defensive distance—the distance similar perhaps to the one that monuments in stone create within the mind viewing them. A monument essentializes and holds static a complex event in time and crystallizes our reactions. The conventional statue of the war general erects a drama within the spectator in which the outsized scale, the very impermeability of the monument, sets in high contrasting relief the viewer's own fragile humanity. Unmistakably, actions are writ large in Glück's work. Turns of thought, hesitations take on portentous meaning and may be read as if they are hieroglyphs of some unfolding, outsized drama. Both the speaker in the poems and the reader may appear simultaneously to engage in this contract of self-distancing and wariness. Glück's speakers, after all, watch themselves as if they are studying specimens. (Of course monuments cannot study themselves or question themselves.) Yet if some readers, like Henry, disparage the autobiographical focus of the poems, one can argue that Glück's defenses reveal a respect for the reader quite unlike that of many of her contemporaries. The steely advancement of her poems asks the reader's ultimate attention and ultimate seriousness. I have argued elsewhere that in some of her poems this effect is due to the tone of certainty, even of what seems like a posthumous accounting of a life's meaning.[6] It is the power of voice more than scene or even argument, finally, that is most evident in these poems. The power of hearing an uncompromising voice sustains our engagement. Robert Pinsky, in *Democracy, Culture and the Voice of Poetry*, reflects on the "solitary voice" in a way that touches on Glück's stylistic signature: "[Poetry] has affinities with all the ways a solitary voice, actual or virtual, indicates the presence of others. Yet as a form of art it is deeply embedded in the single human voice, in the solitary state that hears the other and sometimes recreates that other. Poetry is a vocal imagining, ultimately social but essentially individual and inward."[7] Glück is a poet of inwardness, surely, and such inwardness may be experienced as an expression of self-loyalty, loyalty to a conception of the significance of one life that rotates against the self-suspicion that otherwise informs the poems.

Glück is her own harshest critic and, in turn, answers her critics in a poetry of defense. In "Ancient Text," misunderstanding is mandated for the angels and for her critics, and in "Summer Night" she defends herself from charges that she has failed to remake the lyric: "Desire, loneliness, wind in the flowering almond— / surely these are the great, the inexhaustible subjects / to which my predecessors apprenticed themselves. / I hear them echo in my own heart, disguised as convention." "Summer Night" refers to critics who would cite emotionality, repetitiveness, and her acceptance of certain conventions as her weaknesses, and answers such charges:

Why not? Why not? Why should my poems not imitate my life?
Whose lesson is not the apotheosis but the pattern, whose meaning
is not in the gesture but in the inertia, the reverie.[8]

Increasingly, Glück has come to write a defense of her sensibility as it counters mortality: This sort of reasoning is consciously aimed at self-protection, perhaps, but also at defense of the lyric as an ancient and inexhaustible mode for claiming the dignity of an individual life as a source for meditation. At any rate, the poet who is disparaged can always look to the future for vindication, as she writes in an essay:

> Toward his critics, the artist harbors a defensive ace: knowledge that the future will erase the present. Not all writers possess in equal measure these preoccupations: that they are available at all, psychically, to diminish the force of critical judgment, separates the judgment of published work from the more annihilating judgments which can occur in actual contact.[9]

It is understandable, then, that *The Seven Ages* (2001), Glück's ninth book, amounts in part to a compendium of misunderstandings corrected, the misunderstandings of critics recounted in a dryly ironic and deceptively gentle tone in "Ancient Text." But more important, Glück makes an account of self-misunderstanding. "Style changes when one has got to the end, willingly or not, of a train of thought," Glück has argued.[10] With each book she has explicitly attempted to change style, but her voice imprint is not in the least abraded, nor is a certain attitudinal range, despite what seem now to be temporary remoldings. It is becoming clear that the softening toward human weakness that was evident after *Arafat* has been partial in some ways, a battle hardly quite won. The dream of perfection reasserts itself in Glück's poems—a perfection imaginable because it seeks an essentialized form. The poem may project the imagination of perfection and an ability to grieve over the failure of the perfect to materialize. After all, Glück's poems appear to suggest that the dream of a psychic elevation, an enlarging perfection beyond that of materialism in contemporary culture, is what most needs to be protected. It is far simpler to acquiesce to a vision of the limited and limiting individual or social group than to seek an aspiration toward a new level of dignity that hardly seems compatible with being human.

A poetic persona could hardly appear less sociable than Glück's, but it is that very refusal of sociability that gives us a sense of her poetry's ultimate integrity. Glück is an explicitly resistant poet. She is a poet of uncompromising ideals, only in middle career veering toward a partial and tentative, and now what seems like an unreliable, accommodation to human weakness and imperfection. In such a light, Glück's appointment in August 2003 as Poet Laureate of the United States would seem to be an unusual choice, for the laureate generally takes on a highly public role as advocate for the art. She follows Billy Collins, who held the post in a manner characteristic of the poetry he writes: with charm, wit, and accessibility. But Glück's poems are resolutely, agonizingly private even when most revealing. There is a tonal template of resistance in the poems, even a fierce defensiveness in their grain. Her poems refuse to make us feel better. They complain. They include bitter dramas of betrayal. They are private without being intimate. We overhear a resolute voice or seem caught in its accusatory rachets. In short, the persona Glück has erected appears at odds with at least the common public perception of the laureate's function. Shortly before the laureateship was officially announced, she told *The Washington Post*, "I have very little taste for public forums."[11] She told *The New York Times*, "I feel honored, but I have not sought public life, so that piece of it is unnerving." Characteristically for a poet who has attempted to rework and revise her perceptions regularly, she told the *Times* that she accepted the position because, "I'm in a moment where tranquility needs to be disturbed. My life is too elaborately structured, and if I'm going to change that, I don't get there by saying no."[12]

A certain detachment toward her materials and toward the reader are part of the very fabric of Gluck's verse. A voice may seem repulsed by common affections and wary of public claims of weakness and vulnerability. In an essay she castigates her culture and those who have suffered and voiced their suffering in a way that seems intent on distinguishing herself from the position of sympathizer: "I don't think our society's addiction to exhibitionism and obsession with progress (a narrow myth for triumph) completely explain the ease with which survivors have begun to show their wounds, making a kind of caste of isolation, competing in the previously unpermitted arena of personal shame."[13] At the 1993 baccalaureate address at Williams College she stood before students to talk of the value of suffering rather than celebration: "It is very strange to stand here, wishing you desolation, like the bad fairy at the cradle," she asserted in noting the irony of her position.[14] She has even made a case for opposing conceptions of the utility of her art. "Art is not a service. Or, rather, it does not reliably serve all people in a standardized way. Its service is to the spirit, from which it removes the misery of inertia."[15] In turn, Gluck's earliest imagery relies on areas of physical experience that explore the ways the psyche militates against self-acceptance, particularly in her writing that uses anorexia as a trope. As Elizabeth Dodd argues, "Glück has developed the poem sequence as a means for extended expression built upon reticence, and she has introduced a startling (and apt) metaphor for women artists of the late twentieth century, likening her poetic attitude—what I call personal classicism—to anorexia nervosa."[16] A poet so dedicated to silence, so willing to express unaffiliation and dissatisfaction, a poet so unconsoling and distrustful of affirmation, may seem a strange choice for poet laureate, admittedly, but a choice that for its uncompromising and unexpected character is enlivening—and challenges static conceptions of what a poem or laureate might be.

It is becoming clear by now that Louise Glück wishes to transform our conceptions of passivity and defense. She mounts what seems like a defense of the defensive position. Defense is, in some ways, one of Glück's proper subjects, particularly defense achieved by inserting analytical measures into situations of emotional complexity, as her prose suggests:

> The deft skirting of despair is a life lived on the surface, intimidated by depth, a life that refuses to be used by time, which it tries instead to dominate or evade. . . . In its horror of passivity, it forgets that passivity over time is, by definition, active. There exists, in other words, a form of action felt as helplessness, a form of will that exhibits, on the surface, none of the familiar dynamic properties of will. Fortitude is will."[17]

Even passivity and activity are revised by Glück; she is our self-consciously counterintuitive poet who challenges the more secure conceptions of human agency. She attempts to revise the self-congratulatory notion that is common to many writers: the belief that writing requires courage: "the poet engaged in the act of writing feels giddy exhilaration; no occasion in the life calls less for courage than does this."[18]

In particular she would defend an ideal of unfleshed perfection in an environment hostile to perfection as an aspiration beyond the sensory, beyond consumerism, and without religious ardor. In a culture of overwhelming verbal and visual stimulants, her turning away from representing affiliation or celebration suggests something like an attempt at a survival of austere principles. It's no wonder she describes forebearance as a virtue.

Marianne Moore, as Jarrell noted, was our modernist of armor. Her "armor" was achieved in part through the act of assemblage: assemblage of quotation, descriptive image, and elaborate syllabic patterning. Glück's poetry, in contrast, seems bare of much visual complication; we "hear" her defensive armor as a matter of tone rather than see it as a matter of imagery. And yet the armor of defense is perhaps more immediately evident in her work than in any of the other poets discussed in this book. Glück's speakers express an undeniable disdain at points for ordinary humanness (in the spirit at times of Robinson Jeffers) and a willingness to ward off imperfection, with what seems like an instinct to reject the imperfect. We can probably think of few contemporary poets whose speakers, drawn from autobiography, might utter the following line with so little apparent irony: "I even loved a few times in my disgusting human way" (*SA* 3).

In the pinpoint of the individual are made volatile the charged experiences of generations. Glück can write about her sense of the importance, even the momentousness, of one life, as if that life were impaled on an axis piercing through time. In doing so, she uses self-history analytically in small scale and casts it through allusions that are aligned to grand, mythic structures. For this, as we have seen, the charge of grandiosity can be leveled, but her work is, I believe, more properly a defense of lyric and lyric potential in a culture that makes, in Frost's terms, very little of a diminished thing. She may be an intensely personal poet who draws on her own autobiography, but she increasingly uses herself as the purveyor of what amounts to a cultural analysis and indictment. To assume that her story is everyone's would strike readers as ludicrous. But to assume that in its outlines her analyses of aging and instinct are applicable only to herself may just as readily miss the mark. She defends disgust, anger, repugnance, even embarrassment. The territory of her poems is nearly claustrophobic at points in its compression and unrelenting focus. But the power of Glück's poems depends on their being privy to a position that is willful and truculent. If the poems, she tells us repeatedly, arrive unbidden, and as such are not managed by will, her subject nevertheless is the will itself. She has devoted herself to a poetics of resistance of another sort than Elizabeth Bishop, clearly; where Bishop warps sensory reception just enough to cast light glancingly on the depths of anxiety, Glück builds walls around anxiety by using the intellect—but such walls are always breached. Defenses are never final.

Vernon Shetley addresses the power of an interrogatory position in contemporary poetry in a way that illuminates Glück: "Poetry ought . . . to present its readers with exempla of the kind of mind that continually guards against passing fictions upon itself, that reflects on the operations of its own language and weighs them against a tough standard."[19] Glück's standards are surely high ones. She does indeed cast "fictions" upon the mind, and these fictions are examined and sometimes replaced with new, provisional fictions. It is the self-conscious recognition of these fictions that gives us the difficult and manifold potentials of her poems. One of her most achieved poems, "Arboretum," carried its convictions to a broader public awareness in its criticism of tepidness and mediocrity. Its argument is unexpected: it is the unimpassioned who are greedy and vain, and it is they who rob their children of not simply a model for an engaged and psychologically rich life but of the very possibility to create such a life. The poem begins with "the problem of age, the problem of wishing to linger." She speaks to the enervated characters that we are familiar with from Eliot (one of Glück's early influences) and, as in Eliot, it is their passionlessness that condemns them. While such characters' gardens thrive, "the young / withered nevertheless" (SA 44). In the end "our asking so little for so many years, meant / we asked everything" (SA 45). The note of accusation in the poem is one that she has worked to modulate over the years, focusing a double movement: the accusation that is projected outward returns inward.

For all the suspicion Glück's speakers cast on their own pasts and their own constructions of meaning, her poetry is ultimately defended by the most unbreechable, untheorizable distance: that of the oracular, particularly the mythic oracular. "Before I was three, I was well grounded in the Greek myths,"[20] Glück has written, and myths inform her perspective. She registers the implications of a muted narrative grandeur of implications founded on notions of divine and implacable forces. Glück is a practitioner of what Dodd calls "postconfessional personal classicism—. . . in which the voice of the self is muted by an amplified sense of the mythic, the archetypal . . . without losing the compelling presence of an individual, contemporary 'I,' a personal voice addressing the reader."[21] As Helen Vendler in *The Music of What Happens* points out, "Glück has tried in her poetry to give experience the permanent form of myth."[22] The narrative of myth is a common resource for poetry, but there are many ways to exploit the resource. Glück has stamped her poems from the start with an insistence on aggrievement that is individual yet draws from the mythic, and her poems affirm something very close to the spiritual as it can be rendered outside already defined religious systems. Roberto Calasso in *Literature and the Gods* makes claims for literatures that exalt in a way that suggests Glück's ability to bring into the poem figures and sentiments that are at odds with the deflationary rhetorics of many other poets: "The gods are fugitive guests of literature . . . Every time the writer sets down a word, he must fight to win them back."[23] Glück's poems return repeatedly to questions of nonhuman agency. Perhaps less recognized is how a representation of spatial distance associated with myths of origin is crucial to her poetry. *Descending Figure*, the title of her third book, serves as an image of moving downward from a distant perspective, with great effort, nearly relying on something close to the miraculous to reveal (and not close) the gap between the heights of imagination and the reduction of the agreed-upon real. Perhaps at least as important for Glück as descent is the figure of ascent.

What I want to refer to now is what might be called an annunciatory moment: the moment when a poet discovers an image that encapsulates tremendous conceptual and imagistic energy. The annunciatory moment is unlike others. For a poet who initiates an image that will resonate for years with many aspects of her poetic, the first moment of discovering such an image may be experienced as if it were something close to shock or trauma. What occurs is a new initiation in language. When a poet first invents or discovers the annunciatory effect, whether a syntactic string, a field of events with particular power, or perhaps most often an image that embodies process and relationship, the poet is tempted to repeat the experience. Returning to an inaugural image or event, in other

words, the poet is lured to re-experience, no matter how attenu-
ated, the impact of an initial discovery through subsequent echoes.
If the inaugural impact, the original collision, cannot recur with
anything quite like the first exhilarating jolt to the mind, neverthe-
less the poet's continuing relation to the image offers the compen-
sation of deepening implications, even a tutelage of sorts. What
Susan Stewart has noted in terms of meter can be applied in terms
of imagery: "In the accumulation or accrual of returns to certain
meters, the poet can come to learn *in time* and in an ongoing prac-
tice the deeper structures of his or her own thought and emotion
in relation to the world."[24] The image of impact for Glück appears
to be one in which creating physical distance is enacted, whether
in descent or ascent. She is concerned with creation scenes as an
outgrowth of the rhetorical strategies that her poems evince, strat-
egies which depend on a stripping down of a conception, reducing
it to its earliest origins. Perhaps not surprisingly then, stories of
beginnings interest her and are replicated often in her poems.
What is clear is that the narrative of beginnings is invested with
images of ascending into a distance, particularly ascent that allows
a speaker to make visual discriminations from a distance. In the
poems' workings, genesis is a product of distance, and the creator/
poet is most often the one who surveys productions from on high.
In "Lamentations," from *Descending Figure* (1980), it is this image
of a spectral distance—a perspective so removed that it is posi-
tioned above the earth—that carries the import of discovery for
Glück:

> And from the meaningless browns and greens
> at last God arose, His great shadow
> darkening the sleeping bodies of His children,
> and leapt into heaven.
>
> How beautiful it must have been,
> the earth, that first time
> seen from the air.[25]

The highest invention of this poem rises in perspectival shift in
these final lines. By the time we meet the above lines we have trav-
eled in sequence within the four-part poem from "The Logos" to
"Nocturne" to "The Covenant," arriving at "The Clearing." We

have moved from the word itself, to the word embodied in song, to the word embodied in judicial promise, ultimately to a sweeping away, a space where language and meaning are threatened and where God mounts to heaven with a sudden uprush of energy, breaking the poem's surface. The God poised in the poem is a creature of earth who wakens from earth; his rising shadow is cast over the unconscious forms of humans. Here her speaker puts herself behind God's eyes.

Glück's focus on a divine first sight of earth from above the earth accomplishes at least two things: the image reinforces the conception that humans made God out of need; that is, God arose from earthly, not heavenly, conditions. Furthermore, her image of ascent establishes the paradox that this human-made God must take on independence and vigor: he "leapt into heaven." That is, our conceptions—including the conception of God—ultimately grow and become independent of us. In turn, Glück's final lines remind us of something extraordinary and relatively new in the history of humans: we are among the first humans to see the earth from space. Because of our technological advancements we see "like God." And yet we can never see the earth as if for the first time, with all the startlingness of initial seeing. We put our God up before us; "firstness" belongs to him and not to us. As such, the poem's chains of conceptions are among Glück's more complex: God is earth-born; human beings are both suspended in unconsciousness and, at the same time, through the very structuring powers of language, deigned to be parents of God and, like virtually all of Glück's parental figures, fated to have no real idea of what they have made, or what their creation means. (Children in Glück's poems are rather like little gods themselves, as carriers of an imperious will. In a sense, Glück is revising Stevens who writes, "This happy creature—It is he that invented the Gods."[26] In Glück we might change the descriptive to "unhappy.")

The title of the collection from which this poem is taken, *Descending Figure*, takes on further resonance in light of its final poem series. We are in perpetual descent in the participial mode—and we are descendants of forebears who assembled (here we might think again of Stevens) the language structures surrounding us and moving within and beyond us. After each generation's continual reinvention of God, we are the ones who descend. We have imagined a highest possibility and now can only gravitate downward from the attempt to project absolute perfection. Distance, as such, is profoundly linked for Glück to imaginative agency. To complete the poem is to survey the poem, to see it from a perspective of willed distance.

Glück's greater fluency in recent years has increasingly freed her from the dryly psychoanalytic perspective of *Ararat*. Indeed, her increasing fluency, beginning with *The Wild Iris*, may be a product of middle age. As she creates dialogues with her own work, her responsiveness has grown as her body of work has accumulated. Glück, that is, works by recollection of earlier poems; by courting imagery and conceptions that return (a mild and innocent sister; a beech tree; the stunted kingdom of early youth ruled by an adolescent's disdain; an identity veering between self-inflation and self-destruction). The past is internalized, but may be interpreted, becoming a perceptual channel.

The Seven Ages (2001) is Glück's book most committed to shifting boundaries between immateriality and materiality. "I was human: / I had to beg to descend" (*SA* 3) she writes in the title poem, signaling that she would reverse a continual upward motion toward imagining absolutes in her poems. Glück's self-accusation toward an earlier phase of her development reflects her own struggle to attend to and represent yearnings for exalted and perfect forms. In *The Seven Ages* the word *dream* or a variant occurs nearly two dozen times and the word *distance* occurs at least ten times. "Things became dreams, dreams became things" (*SA* 61). Only imagination allows for possession of the earth. "Earth was given to me in a dream / In a dream I possessed it" (*SA* 4). What she creates here is the sensation of suspension, as if consciousness hovers above earth. The poems shift toward a blending and a dissolution of substance, with dream as origin and end point, dreams merging into dreams, Glück's tempest dissolving into thinner and thinner air.

With a focus on the poet's entering her sixth decade, *The Seven Ages* recirculates Glück's previous texts and dominant images, even as we are explicitly pointed to the melancholy undersong of *The Tempest* where dream, oblivion, and renunciation surge. The book opens with Prospero's invocation to Caliban, "Thou earth, thou, Speak." As such Glück immediately inaugurates a perspective in which mind and body are absorbed at one moment and divided at the next. We may recall that by commanding Caliban as "earth" to speak, Prospero commands his servant to withdraw from the earth. To assume speech is to cast off earth's fetters, to distinguish the self from insensate matter. The oppressed, the repressed, the resistant are commanded to speak. Yet it is Prospero's tone of disdain that we register, a note of disdain toward earth and bodily matter that Glück assumes in her earliest books, with their contempt for and repugnance toward bodily appetites. Likewise, Glück's ninth book as a whole is deeply concerned with inciting voice and the problematics of assuming voice; making the earth speak is to disabuse the earth of being earth. Such a sentiment is one that is familiar, reiterated as it is in much of her poetry. We can trace the inclination back through the earthly body that speaks and the petrified body, a betrayer, a collaborator; and yet a site of power in even her earliest books. Under the "surface" of the poems, the body is resistant to any explanation offered for its wants. The speaker would follow what seems like a glistening path of lengthening time and space, toward which she would aim affection and desire, for the object of desire will not be met. Desire is figured as a moment of ascension, an upward emotional ascension above the daily and the corrupt.

In "Moonbeam" distance is reiterated as an inscripting image. Here the body is horizontalized, and again we turn to origins: "And from out of nowhere lovers came." Glück assumes the reader's restlessness and declares an identity with the reader:

> You are like me, whether or not you admit it.
> Unsatisfied, meticulous. And your hunger is not for experience
> but for understanding, as though it could be had in the abstract.
>
> (*SA* 5)

Her desirous ones want the impossible. Because the distance between lovers cannot be entirely traversed, because intimacy cannot be achieved in her narrative, the object of love is untouched and consequently unsoiled. The one loved, at best, may be longed toward, and longing is for Glück a preferred state. Longing even achieves for the one who longs something like immortality. In "The Sensual World," Glück's speaker wishes for "suspension," but no suspension prevails except that of desire: "You will be damaged and scarred, you will continue to hunger" (*SA* 7). Against an indomitable natural order, what we have is a manipulating of distance arranged against the encroachment of bodily failure. The human are law bound, and the shapes of feelings, the latitudes of being, have been internalized and set. In opposition to laws of aging and death, Glück places poems with their heightening and enlargement of the abstract.

The object of love in Glück's poems has always been just a shade short of a demon lover, and in "Dream of Lust" a young figure would remove the speaker from the world. The proposed lover is a destructive force oblivious to the ordinary whom she must, with mixed feelings, reject: "it is still not worth / losing the world" (*SA* 47). Oddly, the details suggest that the lover may be actual; that it is the actual that destroys "the world," given that the world for Glück, at least in *The Seven Ages*, is most fully experienced or approached through imagination. And yet Glück asks explicitly about the nature of love, citing love as a construct that repeats itself despite the particularities of a partner. A question troubles the collection: Is love a form of the imagination and thus at base an impersonal force, which repeats itself despite human particulars? Is it love as imagination that we desire, and not the lover? Often in the collection it is love "on paper" that takes hold through remembered letters, a correspondence that somehow contains a distance that allows the imagination to continue to reach upward. Aspiration—a species of romantic ambition—animates these poems. Longing is enlivening distance that makes erotics possible in the abstract and inflates ritualized patterns, as "Exalted Image" suggests. The sense of scarcity that underwrites the poems is vitiated when the personae appear at windows or on balconies, unabashed, not simply hungry for grand meaning but defensive about the uses to which the imagination of grandeur is put as it withholds the mundane, as in "The Destination." Tellingly, the beloved is known through voice as muse:

> A few days. Intensity
> that was never permitted to develop
> into tolerance or sluggish affection.

Here erotic relationships are characterized repeatedly by physical and conceptual separation. A romance conducted through letters or through few but intense meetings essentializes the relationship and renders it in the guise of a haunted perfection. It is the lover who, in the form of a voice, makes this transformation into a pure magnetic sphere of intensified meaning possible. As such, we mustn't forget that a voice, while of the body, need not remain with the body. Voices can be enmeshed in the grid of the poem where all of the peculiarities of syntax and diction and rhythm deliver to us the romantic shadow of the irreplaceable individual. Yet a voice is treasured here in part because it can be delivered without a body— through letters, poems, electronic devices. It is erotic feeling without consummation that changes time's contours. It is erotic distance, the unattainable, that compels: "And each meeting charged with a sense of exactness, / as though we had traveled, separately, / some great distance" (*SA* 28).

An unempathetic reader might say that this is the erotics of the crush, and Glück is surely aware of the possible charge. She suggests a respect for the processes of romantic idealization, even if she notes explicitly elsewhere her wariness of romance. What happens in the poems is that romance is translated into the imagination, but such a translation requires the base element of romance and even an initial resistance toward romance, the necessary friction from which the poem is born. At least for Glück much of her most successful poetry appears to be made from reluctance. While Glück's speaker longs for solitude as it allows for reverie, solitude replaces the lover without replacing the sensation of yearning. Eros allows her to be alone and "suspended" as such above common concerns—and it is that state of being which interests her most and which she finds to be most misunderstood. It is the state of being in which the poet may most likely be summoned by the poem.

Much of this poetry is faintly shadowed by troubadour-like expectations. Glück's "The Destination," as we have seen, yearns toward voice, the disembodied voice, the voice of the lover who is distant from the poem's persona. In "The Destination" the speaker is ghosted by memory of a beloved person, now dead, and seen previously only intermittently throughout ten years. This sort of encounter despite, or because of, its frustrations becomes an ideal. There is none of the human messiness, but only the stunning collaboration of the other in the imagination, the beloved unabridged by familiarity. In its implicit dynamics, "The Destination" explores two contexts in abbreviated form: our consciousness of

space and our consciousness of time, with each taking part in a
common rhetorical field. Days are "spread out" and range "over
the course of a decade." Time is made linguistically visible, arrayed
over the field of space through metaphors. Time enters space as
"destination," and destination as space becomes a voice, which is
measured in sound waves and time intervals. Later, feelings would
"extend those days, to be inseparable from them"; time unfolds in
physical dimensions until the poem finally arrives at a still point:
time transformed into material space, into a perfect sphere. The
lover is then transformed entirely into the imagination. It is neces-
sary to recall that the collection from which this poem comes, after
all, is called *The Seven Ages,* and while the book contemplates age
in its different stages it does so dimensionally, converting time into
space and space into time by putting forward the linguistic pene-
trability of concepts dramatized in pairs. But finally it is the erotics
of distance, a strangeness that won't admit familiarity, that allows
Glück a certain apprehension not available otherwise. She writes
of another sort of perception of imaginative possibilities, altering
time by stretching it, and evaporating limits until distance itself be-
comes the erotic object, as we shall see unmistakably in "The
Ruse." The poem clicks down toward a conclusion with its own pe-
culiar distancing effect; she is attracted to an illusion. Yet while she
realizes it is an illusion, she defends the illusion. Her speaker's pre-
ferred eroticism is an imaginative power that occurs without the
lover. The motivating force is an absent beloved, and the experi-
ence of absence is here inherently aesthetic.

It is an erotics of the mind that gratifies. Distance, after all, feeds
the imagination. It is the space between lovers, the unmet, that be-
comes the focus of desire. As Adam Phillips writes, "When Freud
wrote in his *Three Essays on Sexuality* that the object was 'soldered'
on to the instinct, he was saying, in his technical way, that the peo-
ple we desire, the people we are drawn to, are secondary, an after-
thought; that we are simply the bearers of free-floating desire that
is always seeking its targets; that if we are having a primary rela-
tionship with anything, it may not be with other people but with
our own desire."[27] Glück's "The Ruse" extends Phillips's medita-
tions, for it is a poem enacting a choice for "great distances." The
argument of the poem finds in distance itself the object of love:
"erotic passion / thrives on distance" (*SA* 59). After recurrent loves,

what remains is "distance, the servant of need" (*SA* 60). And finally it is not the beloved body, after all, that compelled:

> The eyes, the hands—less crucial
> than we believed. In the end
> distance was sufficient, by itself.
>
> (*SA* 60)

Glück stakes her claim; the actual other disappears. It is finally the conception of the unpossessable that is the love object, distance as motivating abstraction, distance as untheorizable and thus safe from not only critical depredations but her own aesthetic depredations. Imagination is spun about a withdrawal as much as an entrance. It is the distance itself—this felt separation of space and time—that is the origin and end-point of the speaker's feeling. The erotics of the beloved at a distance become an erotics of the imagination, a state analogous to the writing state, a state in which we are not in actual contact with another, in relation, but in which we are in contact with the properties of words as they arrive within the mind.

In Glück a defense of poetry is a defense of defensiveness, refusal, negation, implacability. What Glück does is to concretize the abstracting of distance, to make distance the stable absolute. It is the imagination that provides accuracy of perception. The imagination discovers meaning and achieves what she regards as higher-order accuracy:

> Not to be reclaimed or re-entered
> but to legitimize
> silence and distance,
> distance of place, of time,
> bewildering accuracy of imagination and dream—
>
> I remember my childhood as a long wish to be elsewhere.
> This is the house; this must be
> the childhood I had in mind.
>
> (*SA* 55)

We should note, however, that it is "bewildering accuracy" that this poet alludes to, after all. Tellingly, *The Seven Ages* ends with a fable that registers bewilderment before the endpoint which Glück has reached. As in the conclusion of "Lamentation," a position above a world is assumed, and we must peer downward. The poem is a brief fable of death and of an afterlife of light, of unremitting abstraction. The soul is guided to nirvana, but the soul's response in the glare is to reject what it experiences: "And I said again *But the light will give us no peace*" (*SA* 68).

Linda Gregerson points out that Glück is producing "work that is so impeccably itself that it alters the landscape in which others write while at the same time discouraging (and dooming) the ordinary homage of direct imitation."[28] Glück has indeed succeeded in creating a voice that might be echoed somewhat but not significantly imitated. As Calvin Bedient claims, "With her self-denyingly mannerless manner, she is now writing English in its most purified form."[29] Her poems yearn toward faith without institutional prescriptions by resisting a deflationary meaning and by investing in a defensive rhetoric. In some ways she might recall us to the austere forms of perfection practiced by the contemporary painter Agnes Martin, who has argued that "The function of art work is the stimulation of sensibilities, the renewal of memories of moments of perfection." Glück does not protect weakness so much as she protects the imagination continually abashed by reality.

4

Scholarship and Debasement: Overlaying the Defenses in Anne Carson

> . . . what we are engaged in when we do poetry is error,
> the willed creation of error,
> the deliberate break and complication of mistakes
> out of which may arise
> unexpectedness[1]

"The fact of the matter for humans is imperfection," Anne Carson has written in "Essay On What I Think About Most" (*MOH* 35). In turn, "The fact of the matter" is that imperfection—the failure to meet an ideal—is subject matter for all the poets whose work we have discussed. We have met imperfection in Niedecker's work as she dissolves the image's stability, working through idioms that disrupt the visual plane. We have encountered Bishop's protective environment for her fantastical, playful, perfectly imperfect creatures. Most significantly, we have encountered Glück's resistance to human imperfection before imaginative ideals. But where Glück has taken the imperatives of perfection, Carson has taken the imperatives of imperfection as her generative bedevilment in what amounts to an analysis of imperfection that flaunts its own refusals of exactitude. In Carson the urge toward perfection requires imperfection, requires Keats's lovers never meeting, never kissing. A classics scholar from Canada who imports her disciplinary practices into her poetry, Carson locates scholarship in emotional need. She returns an explicit claim of the searching personal consciousness to the drive for knowledge.

Error, Carson tells us, drawing on Aristotle, is related to metaphor and allows for a heightened awareness, for error "causes the

mind to experience itself" (*MOH* 30). Such mental reflexiveness
makes us lose "our footing." The "smooth surface" under us drops
away, and the mind is afforded a pleasure—that of determining
an error has been committed, followed upon swiftly by the mind's
delighted sensation of a rightness that is self-gratifying: "mistaken-
ness is valuable" (*MOH* 31). Of course Carson's title, "Essay On
What I Think About Most," followed as it is by a lineated composi-
tion, alerts us to an immediate problem of definition; we are put
on guard as to our bearings, a stance we may often find ourselves
in when confronted with this writer's work. Our first questions ap-
pear inevitable. Are we dealing with an essay or a poem? In its rhe-
torical structure, "Essay On What I Think About Most" appears to
be an essay in Montaigne's sense, a trial, an exploration in which
the author revises herself on the page. And yet Carson's "essay" is
lineated as a poem, and its statements are grouped in verse para-
graphs. Furthermore, the piece carries the ghost of meter and the
imagistic cuts and logical irruptions that we are familiar with from
much contemporary poetry. The title then already alludes to
error, an error of designation or an error of appropriation. The
poem begins with two fragments: one noun with a full stop fol-
lowed by another line beginning with a conjunction and ending
with a full stop. The ironies mount, for Carson has created a full
stop dividing what she declares must be joined. We are then given
a timeline for the emotions that accompany error, before, during,
and after the error is committed. After this somewhat dutiful cata-
loguing, the stanza ends with the question "Or does it?"(*MOH* 30)
as if to *undo* certainty and erase belatedly all previous claims. This
sort of Penelope-like unraveling of rhetorical movement is not un-
common in much of Carson's work. It is related to her sense of the
poem as a means of complicating and reinvigorating what we
"mean by meaning." Error spreads; error enlivens in Carson's
poetry. She would make the poem a process of exploration in
which mistakes are fruitful, in which metaphor introduces the
mind to itself. The sensory memory of past effects occludes each
moment—or, alternately, enriches each moment.

As if further to disclose the possibilities of error, the poem fol-
lowing "Essay" constitutes itself as a "draft" of its predecessor.
"Essay On Error (2nd draft)" is shorter, more visceral, and draws
on more historical personages than "Essay," creating wide concep-
tual spaces between references. While "Essay On What I Think

About Most" progresses as if mounting an argument, drawing upon evidence and unfolding its logic, the next poem unfolds without the persuasive ligature of the essayistic poem preceding it. "Draft" referents are deliberately unclear. Descartes, Freud, and Ferenczi are called up, but they seem sentinels to a personal preoccupation. The speaker's comment ascribing herself as the subject of an insult from Freud causes identities to slide and underscores the poem's idiosyncrasy as the pronouns are remarkably unsteady and hardly latched to context. We cannot be sure to whom the antecedents are attached in at least five instances in the twenty-one line poem. The context is unclear as well, but what we do see is that as a companion piece, or as a further redrafting and response to the issues animating the preceding poem, "Essay On Error (2nd draft)" renders the drier, more abstract tone of rhetorical explanation suspect in "Essay On What I Think About Most."

"How people tell time is an intimate and local fact about them," Carson writes in an essay (*MOH* 3). How people repeat themselves is also "an intimate and local fact about them." Her own repetitions—multiple retellings, re-borrowings from her own work, even her interest in Hokusai's daily drawing of lions—betray her attraction to a representation of dimensionality in which time present is layered with time past. To repeat oneself is never ultimately to commit to the same act. We can't step into ourselves twice. She works with the form of a script, director's notes, the actor's reflections on his role, the self-conscious exercise not only in enactment and representation but on method and on reading as a "staging" of the past. She has argued that "An act of reading and writing . . . is an experience of temporal arrest and manipulation."[2] She would make us more conscious of the very effort of reading and of writing, making visible to us the processes of these "sensational crises."[3] Yet for all their far-flung subjects, their ancient, modern, and contemporary personages and texts, and their rehearsals of cinematic structures, her poems stalk their most intimate subjects. They are repetitive in their subtexts, as I shall argue, to the point of obsession.

The pressure of negation in Carson's poems may "create bottomless places for reading" as she says of Simonides of Keos and Paul Celan, setting up a defense against completion. She would disrupt continuities of time and identity, most evidently by her use of techniques imported from film and conditioned by literary devices. As she writes in her discussion of "method" in *Economy of the Unlost*, "To keep attention strong means to keep it from settling. Partly for this reason I have chosen to talk about two men at once."[4] Her poems are inclusive. In "The Glass Essay" alone the images and references mount: a family's dynamics, Emily Brontë's writing, the speaker's love affair, aging and time's depredations, the imprisonment of a stale, caged, unreflective reality. Repeatedly, her poems work across boundaries of genre and time: Carson is a poet of time as it is shelved. She animates poetry with scholarly searches, pulling characters from one period of time into another, or meshing one period or person's line of argument with another's. To call her method juxtaposition hardly does it justice. She works with a suggestive style of interruption in which ancients and moderns coincide and in which sequence is abraded. Much of her poetry is principled on methods of retelling or reinvestigating accounts created in periods and cultures far distant from her own. In an interview with John D'Agata, Carson stated, "Form is a rough approximation of what the facts are doing. Their activity more than their surface appearance. I mean, when we say that form imitates reality or something like that it sounds like an image. I'm saying it's more like a tempo being uncovered, like a movement within an event or a thing."[5] Facts are not principally conceived within images in her poetry so much as they are perceived as energy patterns that may resonate across time.

In "Ordinary Time: Virginia Woolf and Thucydides on War" Carson immediately strikes her first sentence by referring to Thucydides' own beginning: that is, Carson's beginning praises his beginning as she recounts Thucydides' history of the Pelopponesian War and its Athenian and Peloponnesian combatants. It is Thucydides' reckoning of different ways to tell time that she finds especially compelling: "Soon this manifold will fuse into one time and system, under the name of war. But first we see it as hard separate facts" (*MOH* 4). Virginia Woolf's "middle" way of being in the midst of "her own time" compels equally, as Carson interposes an account of Theban error with Woolf's reflections on war and its ontology. Carson's essay is marked by quotations and paraphrases of the two authors, as if these echoes not only speak across vast spans of time, but each "recorder" completes the thoughts of the other. The mark on the wall that generates Woolf's speculation is linked to the ancient walls that are broken in Thucydides' account: "Meanwhile the Plataeans were dismantling their civilization from the inside—digging through the party walls between their houses in order to gather and sally forth in strength against the Thebans. They waited for the blackness before dawn" (*MOH* 5). Images amass color (here an intensifying blackness), a heightened perception of the spatial and of one image drawn against another. Carson's elusiveness and refusal to create resolute closure are also familiar poetic conventions. But that these conventions are deployed in an essay with a loosening movement of logic—a logic of unfolding juxtapositions—would seem to refocus our attention; we come to war on a slant. We come to imagine war as the circular, widening devourer of flesh, the duplicitous actuality which we try our best to arrest by anchoring ourselves in a language of identity and representation. "The rapidity of life" is a matter of multiple perspectives suddenly flaring and then tragically collapsing into what appears to be an inevitability. Thus, Carson's double negative of multiple referents (ancients and moderns, and disparate personalities, quotations, and language fields) proves an overlay of forms of knowing embodied in the field of the essay as poem, or the poem as essay.

The book from which this essay is drawn, *Men in the Off Hours,* begins with an attack that is successfully rebuffed. By following the track of an ancient and a modern account inflected by war, the essay ends with the naming of a stain. It begins, then, with defense and ends with nomenclature—but disappointing nomenclature, for the essayist is bothered by the simple declaration of identity. A stain on the wall is not only a stain on the wall but an imperfection that sets the mind alight. Misattribution opens the path to discovery.

Of course the subject of war is the subject of defense and offense. The Plataeans defended their city in Thucydides' account through rough subterfuge and inciting slaughter—by breaking through their own houses. That is, they destroyed what was theirs to protect, their own boundaries. If we assume the metaphor of language as in some ways our house—a Heideggerean metaphor—Carson would defend the imagination here by making a channel, drawing through boundaries to take up an offensive position. But in some ways it is Virginia Woolf who, in actuality, is given the last word, suggesting that awareness in inspired writing somehow must be kept secret, even from a beloved. Carson narrates the moment of adopting a defensive disguise, after Woolf has "flown" in intense concentration into the realms of imaginative language and subsequently hides her pleasure from her husband: "'I drank my milk and concealed my excitement'" (*MOH* 8).

Peter Quartermain notes in another context "the recurrent collision in twentieth-century American poetics is between semantic singularity and multiplicity."[6] The collision continues into the twenty-first century in some poetry where there seems little semantic singularity to be had. We might think of poems as arrayed along a spectrum of multiplicities. And yet a poet like Carson complicates our perspective, for while her poems appear committed to multiplicity in reference and form, to axes of meaning and generic porousness, what remains especially interesting about her poems is their ability to allow the singular kernel of an obsessive story of betrayal to reemerge. In the midst of the cross-hatching of genres, languages, time periods, perspectives, and cultures, she prefers mixed and divided states of thinking and feeling uttered in bewildering aphorism.

What distinguishes Carson from her predecessors and contemporaries is that she would not only merge genres, the poem and the scholarly article or essay, and historical, mythological, and literary figures, as if time could be interpenetrated or even reversed at any point, but that neither the scholarly techniques nor the excesses of passion, including the most obsessive and deluded passions, are abraded in her work. Indeed, both are used in the service of what she calls the "tempo" of large abstract themes. Even narratives of romantic betrayal would seem illuminated at some moments within the grand theme of time, for betrayal is a kind of dislocation of time, a breaking of continuity. That is, a promise broken makes us reconsider time, reverse our expectations, see newly the past and attempt to spot the genesis of treacheries. In an interview Carson comments that she is fascinated by "classical texts which are, like Sappho, in bits of papyrus with that enchanting white space around them, in which we can imagine all of the experience of antiquity floating but which we can't quite reach. I like that kind of surface."[7] The surfaces of her own poems are riddled with silence points as well as paradoxes that make us confront our most common conceptions because of the very boldness of her ability to collapse representations of time and space, to usher the ancient dead and the modern dead and living contemporaries into one space and synchronous time. Carson's reflections on Plato are especially telling in this context:

> Plato's analogies are not flat diagrams in which one image (for example, gardens) is superimposed on another (the written word) in exact correspondence. An analogy is constructed in three-dimensional space. Its images float one upon the other without convergence: there is something in between, something paradoxical: Eros.[8]

We might pay special attention to the double colon in Carson's final sentence, above: the independent clause poised between the first colon and the second performs as an interruption, a syntactic mirroring of the function she ascribes to eros.

It seems undeniable that Carson's discipline and practice as a classicist contours and conditions her poetry. But the very fact that her poetry is indebted to and spun out of scholarship invites resistance, for the animating argument in which emotion and intellect are inherently divided continues to be an irritant in contemporary discussions of poetry, whether or not that division is explicitly addressed. To some scholars, Carson's unconventional methods would seem erratic and overly personal. She is accused of overreaching or of being "naïve" (as she has noted). For critics of poetry, her scholarship as it animates her poetry may be troubling in other ways. David C. Ward, for one, criticizes Carson as yet another agent of "modernism's driving force: appropriation"[9] and accuses her of "a tic of scholarship; she cannot resist showing off her erudition." He closes his article by wishing otherwise and setting up a scene in which "she scrapes away the lacquer of her erudition."[10] Carson's conjectural erudition is not, however, an incidental aspect of her poetic but inherent; it is a source of subject matter and process. The processes of research and its promises, the questioning of interpretations and etymology, the advancement of tentative theses, the examining of conceptualizations in different language systems: these disciplined acts are inextricable from much of her poetry. Not only are these acts a subject and a practice but a form of motivation; they evince mental and emotional drives as exhilarating habits of mind. Her method implicitly asks the question: why should we ever deny the farthest reaches and methods of inquiry—of many sorts of inquiry—to our poetry?

The pleasures we take in Carson diverge in some ways from those we take from the other poets discussed in this book. Glück's poems, for instance, provide us with pronouncements, even when those pronouncements are ambiguous. Her poems provide us with models of raising experience to an archetypal status. Her poems inform us that they matter—even if some critics purposefully resist the summons. Carson, on the other hand, catches what appear to be personal stories with an autobiographical basis in the densest textual circuits of other narratives and interpretive systems. As Carson has argued about her fascination with Greek language and texts, "We have to decide between *and* and *either/or*. For them [the Greeks] they're just two sides of one coin—as soon as you think into that fact you realize that the world could be completely other than it seems. There are a lot of those little things in Greek. I wouldn't feel confident saying there are quantitatively more, but there are a lot of those moments where you enter a fact but then you just think, 'Oh, there's a whole other way to look at this element of reality,' and then you think of the world through that lens for a while and everything is slightly different."[11] As she acknowledges in the same interview, the structures of her poems emerge because no form seems adequate. She admits her own frustration: "I think the forms are in chaos. I seize upon these generic names like *essay* or *opera* in despair as I'm sinking under the waves of possible naming for any event that I come up with."[12]

At points, Carson's poetry gives the illusion of explaining itself. But part of its difficulty is that it is relentlessly broad in allusiveness, sometimes scholarly in tone, and at the same time beset by passions that we are unaccustomed to seeing in contemporary poems that wear their cerebral pedigree so overtly. Scholarship is, we should note, personal for Carson, a means to re-envision the most persistent emotional conflicts. Her essays, included in her poetry collections, augment the poems rather than extend their arguments. They certainly do not explain the poems. To the essay she brings the poem's uncertainty, the visceral image, a structure that may be circular in its concerns. The structure of Carson's narratives in poetry or essays is complicated not only because of the multiple contexts in which stories of betrayal appear but because of the story kernel's stubbornness. Her speakers' initiatory moment is in rejection: "It is stunning, it is a moment like no other, / when one's lover comes in and says I do not love you anymore."[13] Most frequently, Carson writes in defense of erotic narratives of abasement, and the poems reenact that narrative compulsively. As Elaine Scarry writes, "Those who remember making an error about beauty usually also recall the exact second when they first realized they had made an error."[14] Carson's poems are struck by the stubborn seductiveness of beauty and an absolute dismay when the one we believe to be most beautiful abandons us.

A defense of poetry in Carson's terms is a defense of error. And thus a really good defense of poetry is a defense of repeated errors. And what is a bad love affair but an error?

What can be learned from such an error? Carson writes a poetry that enacts experiences of need and loneliness, so that the overplus of language and reference creates a tension against the self-shrinkage and self-abandonment we associate with shame. Her voice, striate, suddenly intimate, seemingly defended by scholarly procedures at many points and then exposed, moves from quick runs in etymology and leisurely scholarly ruminations to hermetic lyric utterances. In the midst of such diverse rhetorical momentums, Carson's poems recast scenes, revisiting and recontextualizing a central drama in which desires are frustrated repeatedly in love. Her poems appear to build a skin of scholarly reference, at the center of which is the image of, or allusion to, a woman who has been betrayed cruelly and without reason. That is, the poems often hold up the authority of specialized knowledge, crossing lyricism with the contours of the most rigorous scholarship. But at the inner layers of the poem is a cry of betrayal and romantic need, and within that cry is a stirring note of abasement.

Generally, the narratives of betrayal in many of Carson's poems are alike. The dynamic may be heterosexual, although not always (as in *Autobiography of Red*), and yet the object of love tends to be male. Most often a woman loves a man who is mysterious in some ways, remarkably self-absorbed (his absorption extends outward at most to war games or esoteric scholarship). The beloved man has, or will have, other lovers. He debases the woman about whom Carson's poems revolve in multiple ways and seems to enjoy his displays of power over her. He may steal from her. The woman is abandoned by him through language that is all the more wounding for its banality, even if the speaker can somehow trace to Kafka a parallel: "Not enough spin on it, said my true love / when he left in our fifth year" (*MOH* 12). We may find that the line is connected to Carson's prose in which she notes that a character in Kafka's fiction is angered when a top stops spinning.[15] We may conflate Carson's line about the end of a love affair with Kafka, but reading Kafka doesn't quite soothe heartbreak or make the speaker's rejection any less horrifying, despite its literary pedigree. In such poems, a failure to love is most often a failure to recognize a woman's unique humanness. The woman may then abase herself to court the man's attention, but even sexual promise proves illusory. The husband or lover is in one way or another unable to satisfy himself or to soothe the woman.

Shame arises from "the presence of someone right up against me," Carson has written. It is the awareness of separateness and intrusion. And yet shame—like error in this poetry—is not to be avoided ultimately. "Realizing you've made an error brings shame and remorse," she writes in "Essay On What I Think About Most" (*MOH* 30). Drawing on Aristotle she recasts error, which brings shame, for its potential as "the deliberate break and complication of mistakes / out of which may arise / unexpectedness" (*MOH* 35). The blush of shame between potential lovers alerts them to their very sympathies. Each is brought into greater contact with his or her defining differences.

In "The Glass Essay" the moment of shameful revealing takes on concrete form. The man the protagonist loves says he does not want to have sex with her. Nevertheless, the speaker takes off her clothes and turns her back to him: "he likes the back / he moved onto me." That he prefers her back suggests he prefers not to be seen by her or to look into her eyes—a movement to make meaning emblematic:

> Everything I know about love and its necessities
> I learned in that one moment
> when I found myself
>
> thrusting my little burning red backside like a baboon
> at a man who no longer cherished me.[16]

In Carson a focus on the body is particularly insistent as we read the "backside"—here, the rejected body. The volition in the above lines is presented as if it occurs outside the speaker's will. She "found" herself in this act rather than performed with a sense of agency. She would be then, to herself, a creature of instinct— desperate to be touched even after being rejected. Yet in Carson's scene, rejection constitutes the endurance of a kind of knowledge. That the woman who likens herself to a baboon immediately moves on to a consideration of the soul followed by thoughts about her orgasms and her lover's impotence reflects her terrible loneliness and sense of failure. The encounter can hardly be redeemed, even if we recall a biblical allusion in another poem, "Book of Isaiah": "Isaiah walked for three years naked and barefoot with buttocks uncovered / to the shame of the nation."[17]

A story of lack of fulfillment and of betrayal keeps being told in Carson's poetry. She writes poetry about a distance that reappears. Finally her poems limn obsessive terrain: the understory of a yearning woman or man's betrayal reasserts itself as the intervening images, facts, and quotations remain in circulation or suspend the act of betrayal. Indeed, past narratives in which erotic suffering operates are reenacted through reading experiences and the translation involved in reading. The moment most likely to be confessed in this poetry is interpreted through scholarship. We might think of this poetry as somehow rather like a form of confessional reading or confessional scholarship; the reading flares and is charged with what is unappeasable—not simply the urge to make meaning of human unfaithfulness but to create layers of experience that do not domesticate lived experience so much as allow it to occupy memory in a way we align with texts. It is the imagination that is a passionate affiliate: "Imagination is the core of desire. It acts as the core of metaphor."[18] Our errors are creative; our imperfections are our creations. Carson's crossovers and overlays of media, of representations of time and space, are invested with notes of urgency, distress, embarrassment, and shame. The poems would hardly be possible without the legacy of confessionalism, and yet they enter into a labyrinth in which meaning is not found in the personal without the intervention of the scholarly. The confessional and the scholarly—two modes traditionally at odds, by virtue of the distance they assume between subject and author, author and reader—are here interposed.

What I hope may be most convincing: Carson enlivens contemporary North American poetry by a return to the narrative of desire placed within the colliding frames of poetic experiments. That the narrative of rejection is hardly disguised contributes to her poetry's power. The error is in human relations, and it is a stubborn error. Her poetry, even in its most sensorially focused depictions, balances on a self-conscious awareness of absences. As Carson claims, "Eros is an issue of boundaries. . . . But the boundaries of time and glance and I love you are only aftershocks of the main, inevitable boundary that creates Eros: the boundary of flesh and self between you and me. And it is only, suddenly, at the moment when I would dissolve that boundary, I realize I never can."[19] Lovers must perceive a division, a gap that affords each a magnified sense of what he or she is not. Carson reflects on obsession among the ancients, particularly the Greeks, in their focus on "the crucial importance of boundaries, both personal and extra-personal, as guarantors of human order."[20] But it is this transgression through the erotic, through and "beneath" what she calls "the skins of rituals and individuals both"[21] that concerns her in contemporary relations. It is not unusual, after all, for Carson to invest the world of theory with fleshiness. She probes the line between what goes on inside the body and what occurs outside the body and writes of our vulnerability to the invisible—to mental, physical, and emotional events that go on without our being able to see them. "Actions go on in us, / nothing else goes on. While a blurred and breathless hour / repeats, repeats" (*MOH* 21).

What we work with here is an erotic passion—which is no easy subject for a writer who is a woman to succeed in conveying without amassing some level of rebuke. In the early twentieth century, after all, we had before us the intensities of adulation and revulsion prompted by poets such as Edna St. Vincent Millay and Sara Teasdale. And although their reputations were reconsidered in the final two decades of the past century, the "new woman" and the weight of sexual passion achieved a dated celebrity and exacted a long-term revulsion from at least three generations of poets.

Carson argues that what sustains the erotic is a third party: "For, where eros is lack, its activation calls for three structural compo-

nents—lover, beloved and that which comes between them."[22]
What is animate in the triangle is eros itself:

> Triangulation makes both present at once by a shift of distance, replacing erotic action with a ruse of heart and language. For in this dance the people do not move. Desire moves. Eros is a verb.[23]

In Carson the boundaries of the erotic triangle keep her lovers from entirely making a connection, and the figure of the triangle is linked to her technique of "rotating" multiple narratives over and against one another. Tellingly, in an interview she noted the prevalence of volcanoes in her work and her penchant for painting them. "A healthy volcano" she writes in *Autobiography of Red*, "is an exercise in the uses of pressure."[24] The volcano itself is a kind of triangle, and its interior power intrigues as a figure for sexual obsession. In her essay, "The Gender of Sound," Carson links the voice to an interior that may suggest a volcanic metaphor as well: "Every sound we make is a bit of autobiography. It has a totally private interior yet its trajectory is public. A piece of inside projected to the outside."[25] And yet desire itself is not ultimately within us. "Desire . . . is neither inhabitant nor ally of the desirer."[26] It is, in another of her formulations, a narrative: "Eros is always a story in which loved, beloved, and the difference between them interact."[27] It is this difference and its figuration in distance that—as in Glück—becomes a vital concern. As Carson reflects in *Autobiography of Red*, "'How does distance look?' is a simple direct question / it extends from a spaceless / within to the edge / of what can be loved."[28] What is continually reflected would be the obstruction necessary to eros, for which the keenly felt boundary must be erected. A version of this boundary is in "shamefastness," and our very interest in such a boundary amounts, she writes, to "anthropology": "This science of man, which is always about other people, whose details are exotic, calms us and opens out the further possibility of anthropologizing ourselves. Hence modern love."[29]

In modern love, "crises of touch" are replicated:

> As members of human society, perhaps the most difficult task we face daily is that of touching one another—whether the touch is physical, moral, emotional or imaginary. Contact is crisis.[30]

That intimation of crisis animates the poem, for even when her
lovers touch they may immediately find that a third party inter-
poses—or at least the ghostly suggestion of a seductive other per-
son to whom one of the parties will soon travel. Let me cite a
portion from *Plainwater* that might be the partial representative of
the narrative of the triangle:

> After the first night I slept at his house, which, as you know and he
> does not, is the first night I slept at any man's house. Through the wet
> grass, walking behind him. All of a sudden he stops and bends aside.
> Snaps off a single dark red dahlia, my eyes going out of me like a cry.
> Lover, I thought. Now he keeps going and reaches his car and jumps
> in, placing the dahlia on the seat beside him, drives off. With a wave.
> My car is parked farther down the street.[31]

In this drama, a Eurydice of sorts follows an indifferent and
feckless Orpheus. What we intuit is the woman's desire as she
wishes it to be replicated. The dahlia she expects from her lover
would symbolically confer love. The word *lover* would denote them
both, and present for them both a new identity. But the distance
between word and thing is shown dramatically at the moment
when the ghost of another woman hovers, for to whom does the
man expect to give the flower? The speaker and her lover leave in
separate cars. This anecdotal prose poem operates as a miniature
scenario that holds the key players of the obsessive drama Carson
circulates in much of her work: a desirous person (whether the
wife of *The Beauty of the Husband* or Geryon of *Autobiography of Red*),
a fickle man whose actions are misread repeatedly as symbols (and
whose actions ultimately may not derive as much from fecklessness
as from calculated cruelty), and the final separation of the desiring
lover and the desired through different "vehicles." That is, the lov-
ers will be "conveyed" by seemingly irreconcilable ways of thinking
and behaving. At the heart of the narrative rests some turn on lan-
guage itself; the language of one lover is not fulfilled in the lan-
guage of another. In turn, the hint of some sort of thievery
emerges even in the brief extract cited above; for to the woman the
dahlia is in some ways her due. That the lover has driven off with
it before she has even arrived at her own car is a trope of abandon-
ment, the man's merry wave a punctuation that trivializes the
speaker's own desires.

The armature of scholarship should be the source of authority in Carson's poems, and certainly some critics have questioned if this poet isn't too comfortable with intellection, as if, when anxiety strikes, it's time to bring on Thucydides. While Carson has the philologist's and the classicist's authority, I'm not sure that her authority as a poet resides in intellection, in research itself, in the materials which tend to be unstable for her, sources for pondering and inherently unstable, no matter how much those materials (and the processes of scholarship) are inextricable from her poems. Her authority may more fully reside in a bold act of ligature between scholarship and at least the tonal quality of confession as her scholarship protects the story of romantic triangulation from closure. Surely the scoundrels whom the lovers seek in her poems are determined to be scoundrels, if seductive ones at that. We can be certain of the fact. But the imperatives behind the betrayed partner's compulsions are mysterious. Where Louise Glück's speaker will attempt to bat away sensual demands and to find fault with the beloved in the flesh, or to ascend to a realm of dream, imagination, or myth when confronted with intractable and imperfect flesh, in Carson the lovers' case is complicated by mixed desires. It is not the imagination itself which is the beloved for Carson but something that we might refer to as the soul. Yet that the soul would choose such a flimsy and deceiving vehicle to inhabit as the beloved who appears in these poems is yet another conundrum. The poems may seem like obsessive retellings of a failure in love and separation. We have met these characters before; they are familiar to us, even slightly embarrassing, perhaps, to some readers. Yet the beloved is so theorized in the poem as to be held and contained. Carson's narrators know their own errors and foolishness. They assume authority through their knowledge of their errors, living through error that creates enhanced realizations—and it is a path that links scholarship with love and attempts to collapse distinctions between the two.

It is telling that in *The Beauty of the Husband* we first meet the titular husband through a letter, from him, which the female speaker meticulously analyzes for motivations. The speaker attends to his letter as she might a literary close reading, repeating her primary strategy for understanding. But here repetition is inextricable from infatuation and obsession—repetitive thoughts, repetitive expectations. We are directed in the collection to the husband's stealing of his wife's written work. The fact that he has stolen her attention, her time, and her love means that forms of abuse and denigration are being studied as repeated errors in intimacy.

While Louise Glück's speakers engage in amplified reveries in which they imagine the possibility of a romantically essentialized lover, Carson's speakers long for more common contact and grieve at its loss and feel something close to shame even while they explain away shame. As Carson writes in *Eros the Bittersweet*: "*Aidos* ('shamefastness') is a sort of voltage of decorum discharged between two people approaching one another for the crisis of human contact, an instinctive and mutual sensitivity to the boundary between them."[32] She goes on to state that, "The static electricity of erotic 'shame' is a very discreet way of marking that two are not one."[33] Eroticism, as she tells us often, demands and reveals distance. In Glück, on the other hand, sex is not erotic; it is mind-fettering or mind-emptying. What is most erotic is her persona's yearning transformed into imaginative energy. Glück's speaker hardly has the opportunity to be rejected. The other has already been rejected as human; it is the conception—abstract, out of sensory field—that is sought. But in Carson the erotic bears the risk of rejection and betrayal. The woman in her poems asks to be desired. In contrast, Glück's speaker may ask not to be desired, and even not to desire. In Carson's *Eros the Bittersweet* "Beauty spins and the mind moves."[34] The poem accumulates, disperses. The "pollen" of feeling cannot settle.

"I will do anything to avoid boredom," Carson writes in the first prose poem of *Short Talks*, incorporated into *Plainwater*.[35] In a sense, her poems act out that avoidance repeatedly. The shapes her thinking takes are numerous: reversals, questions, oppositions, logical revaluing. But it is eros that makes disappearance felt. In these poems the departing lover animates a distance, and erotic acts tend to be sudden intrusions on the page. The most avid sex partner is lonely in the moment of sexual congress or finds him or herself attached to a phantom. Even the completed act is begun or interrupted by a fantasy of betrayal. The loved other ultimately seems an exemplar of the elusive fabulations of poetry itself, of a radical instability that only magnifies rather than dampens erotic feeling. The images and sequences of her poems seem purposefully incongruent. Her reflections on Platonic analogies might de-scribe her own practices. The poems, filled with self-betrayal, with an acceptance of a casual cruelty delivered by the loved one, are created to overflow their structures, to betray their own forms.

In Carson, degradation makes for a long memory. She would incorporate allusions in the poems to transmit sensations of elu-siveness; an allusion always at least partly eludes us, flashing before us ranges of erudition. In writing of romantic love through her allusions she has made conscious links to the kinds of thinking that poetry enacts and provokes in clarified form: "The same subter-fuge which we have called an 'erotic ruse' in novels and poems now appears to constitute the very structure of human thinking. When the mind reaches out to know, the space of desire opens and a nec-essary fiction transpires."[36] This circuit runs from and toward the reader but finally transcends our affair with words: "Your absence from the syntax of my life is not a fact to be changed by written words."[37]

The Beauty of the Husband: A Fictional Essay in 29 Tangos (2001) is Carson's most fully realized work to dramatize triangulation, the self-abasement of shame, and the moving force of the erotic. The book's title announces Carson's foraging among and between the genres of fiction, essay, and lyric poetry. The book-length poem, which reflects on metaphorical and actual thievery, was composed after an actual burglary at Carson's apartment, while the poet was teaching at the University of California. After the burglary she was left with only one CD, a tango. "I played it every day and I got tango in my head."[38] As she points out, "once you get into the dance you have to dance it to the end. There's no way out. There's no way to change the steps. It's set. I shouldn't say that every mar-riage is like that, but romantic expectations are like that. . . . There are certain rules that are made, they lead to other rules, and before you know it the dance is on."[39]

The Beauty of the Husband responds to Keats, who is the volume's explicit guardian spirit and whose words preface each tango. The conundrum that animates the book is drawn from his writing: For Keats, if truth is beauty, what do we do with a beautiful liar? Sur-render, apparently, for it is Keats's line, "GENERAL SURREN-DER TO BEAUTY," which she cites. Comically and coincidentally, the Library of Congress subject area cataloguing for the book constitutes a compression of the volume's story. The listings are arranged in threes (the number of the triangle) on the copyright page, as follows: "1. Married people—Poetry. 2. Marriage—Poetry. 3. Adultery—Poetry."

The narrative core of *The Beauty of the Husband* is familiar to Carson's readers; we've seen this story appearing at some level in many of her poems. The beloved here is pointedly yet again a thief, not only of a woman's trust but of her art, her written record of their relationship. He is most particularly a thief of words. After sexual intercourse, the man steals the woman's writing. Ironically enough, the piece is titled "On Defloration." (There is indeed a talk in "Short Talks" by that title which reads in part: "And when you dishonored me, I saw that dishonor is an action."[40]) The husband's words are malicious, his letters entice and wound. The speaker's note that "The divorce decree came in the mail"[41] suggests as well the husband's staggering role as a sender of painful messages even from afar. And yet Carson presents him as a force allied to poetry, surely to a disruptive poetry of doubleness and fabulation. The husband, then, is the lover as Hermes, and the wife measures obsessively what he has stolen: "5820 elegaics," "53 wirebound notebooks" "[p]iled on four shelves in the back kitchen," "maybe a night and a day and a night to read through" (*BH* 125). Here the act of counting what is missing amounts to a pun. We count objects; a man can be counted on, or a man can't be counted on. The bulk of what he has stolen is measured in terms of time and space and form and placement, meticulously remeasured just as Carson declares Thucydides tells time—in multiple ways. The husband seemingly inhabits her imagination, and his most stirring response to her occurs at his grandfather's farm after a round of grape stomping, as if he were suddenly playing the part of Dionysus on demand. It comes as a surprise to learn then that the couple's marriage is not fully consummated for six months, as if the principle of delay and interruption must be at work continually in each area of their lives. Of course we may identify with the female speaker's desire, but not with her desire for this particular man.

We might ask, even in a first encounter with the husband, if we are dealing with a man or an archetype. Both, it seems. In *The Beauty of the Husband* the husband is adept at war games (the marriage itself is a war game), stealing property, and crass manipulation. Yet he is a liar for largely senseless reasons. Unlike an Odysseus whose lies strategically allow for his survival and whose clever tricks ultimately propel him toward the object of his one faithful desire, the husband in Carson's narrative poem is a reverse-Oedipus, as the reference to Keats's famous coupling of truth and beauty is manipulated. The man is beautiful—without any allegiance to truth—unless we entertain truth as inherently shifting, disloyal, and elusive (surely more than a possibility for Carson: a conviction). Her narrative in its implications about falsehood veers close to Elaine Scarry's suppositions:

> This liability to error, contestation, and plurality—for which "beauty" over the centuries has so often been belittled—has sometimes been cited as evidence of its falsehood and distance from "truth," when it is instead the case that our very aspiration for truth is its legacy. It creates, without itself fulfilling, the aspiration for enduring certitude. It comes to us, with no work of our own; then leaves us prepared to undergo a giant labor.[42]

The husband's (now ex-husband's) assumption into normalcy completes the volume. He at last speaks as a remarried man and a father of two, seemingly immersed in the ordinary. Yet despite the years he is again guilty of larceny. We know that he reads his former wife's letters at the funeral service of their mutual friend Ray. In the twenty-eighth tango the italicized lines quote from a letter that offers one of his most developed takes on things:

> *My philosophy of life is that everything is as it seems—*
> *at a distance. Tanks on the edges of forests.*
> *Tanks on the edges of forests.*
>
> (*BH* 134)

The letter is lugubrious and portentous and reflects a man happy to befuddle the letter's recipient as a way to gain the upper hand. Yet the woman who loved him must discover that what she searched for has its original within her. Her imagination creates an idealized image of the beloved. And yet ultimately she may come to see desire as internalized and that she must recognize her own defenses. The now ex-wife must discover a distance herself, in an echo of the key word in his letter to her:

That the beautiful when I encountered it would turn out to be
prior—inside my own heart,
already eaten.

. . . .

Inside. He was already me.
Condition of me.

(BH 140)

The heart is eaten; like Persephone the speaker has consumed new
knowledge. If we are betrayed, we may experience the world as
lacking texture, heft, weight. What we "possess" has no more sub-
stance than a dream, seemingly less, as deception overwhelms
inner experience and is replayed upon outer experience. What is
left but the wish to honor the erotic force as it is animated before
us?

Distance—this foregrounded gap—is evoked in Carson as a de-
fense, a boundedness that inspires erotics and compels its recogni-
tion. In *Autobiography of Red*, a conversation focuses on a sensory
"hold" or perception of distance in time that is applicable to Car-
son's unfolding understanding of defensive boundaries:

. . . That is who we are. Creatures moving on a hill.
At different distances, *said Geryon.*
At distances always changing. We cannot help one another or even cry out—[43]

Surely the question of "who we are" baffles Carson. As Harriet
Zinnes has said, "The self is there [in the poetry] but not arrogant,
and more elusive than narcissistic."[44] Carson herself has said in an
interview with John D'Agata, "I don't like thinking about myself, I
don't like thinking about who I am. It's like watching yourself
walk. You inevitably stumble."[45] In the same interview she refers to
herself as "a set of facts."[46] In the "Who's Who" section after her
translations of Sappho, Carson heads the list with the following:
"Abanthis: woman about whom nothing is known."[47] Early in her
career Carson almost worked to make the same true of herself in
giving relatively few interviews and by insisting on the briefest au-
tobiographical material on the dust jackets of her books. But of
course her poems and essays are inscribed with more than a set
of facts. They are inscribed recognizably by an idiosyncratic mind

studying obsessive materials as a means of making discoveries of magnitude, even while defending the vulnerabilities we are prey to in the midst of recalcitrant mysteries and the questions those mysteries compel us to ask. Or, as Carson titles the first poem of *Plainwater*: "What Is Life Without Aphrodite?"

Afterword: The Price We Pay
for Making Claims

To make a claim means to tease its opposite into the open. That is the price we pay for making claims. Reading defenses may mean that what is protected is actually newly marked, encircled, targeted for attention and brought to the surface to be exposed. A poem may appear to defend vulnerabilities, but to defend vulnerabilities may increase their visibility. We know what another values because of what she most faithfully defends. When Elizabeth Bishop wrote, "It's evident / the art of losing's not too hard to master / though it may look like (*Write* it!) like disaster,"[1] she was creating an autobiography of losses and an injunction about writing: One may write losses not only as inscriptions but as repetitive inscriptions. One writes interrupted similes, for the comparisons we make afford us only temporary, provisional alliances, a possibility that even her parenthesis suggests visually, for a parenthesis may look like an incomplete defensive boundary.

As Hélène Cixous asserts, "there is no 'conclusion' to be found in writing."[2] A poem may repel advances about its ultimate meaning by partly enclosing its own contradictions, while something of the excessive, even the excesses of defensiveness, attracts us. A poem does things to time, not only giving us in some cases the illusion of holding time, although other poets may wish us to experience time as a process, but transforming, or even reconstituting our experience of time. A defense of poetry is at points a defense of experiences cast in an alternate time. We are not out of time so much are we are manipulating the fictions of personal and historical time.

I have suggested here that many poems are set up with lines of defense. Such poems compel us to think of questions of authority and vulnerabilty, even conducting an end run around certain difficulties of stereotyping faced by the poet who is a woman; that is, the physically permeable sex is expected to take defensive measures against violation. That the writers we have discussed choose defensive measures is not simply reflective of temperament but of their cultural position. They constitute their own defenses in their poetry itself, and trouble our sense of assertion as well as defense.

We might turn now to the Irish poet Eavan Boland. In her poetry, essays, and interviews, Boland has frequently set out a scene that is illustrative of the way a poet's first practices haunt her later discoveries. Boland refers to her time in a London flat when she discovered in her own annunciatory moment how to write poems:

> I can see it [the flat] now, and I have wanted the reader to see it. It was not large. It looked north rather than south. The window beside the table was small and inclined to stick on rainy afternoons. And yet for me, as for so many other writers in so many other rooms this particular one remains a place of origin.[3]

Boland repeats variants of this scene of the place where she first began writing in *Object Lessons* in such essays as "In Search of a Language," in "Turning Away," and in "Subject Matters." The scene is echoed in her poems "Domestic Interior," "The Women," "Nocturne," "Code," and "Is It Still the Same." In her extended treatments she presents the romance of the woman writer in close-up. In the scene, a young woman, most often at dusk, sits alone at a desk. She is writing, or alternately, reading. But if she is reading, it is with a writerly attention, so attentive that she seems to be a partial inventor of the text before her, reading/writing a poem into being. Most often the scene takes place in what Boland calls that "in-between-time" of dusk, a "shape-shifting time," as the emergent poet engages in an almost ritually focused activity. We gain an impression of profound enclosure but also a realization of an outer vista framed by a window. The scene, as such, is framed within a frame.

When a poet returns relentlessly to a scene we can make numerous conjectures. We might speculate that the poet is returning to an unresolved site—to pain or grief. But we might plot the return in terms of pleasure as well. We can say that the return is most likely productive; it is generative. The scene is no longer a recollection of the actual so much as the construction of a developing attitude toward perception. As Helen Vendler writes of Emily Dickinson, "the difficult idea and the solitary prowess in the quiet room came first."[4] The remembered location, colored by intention and will, desire, failure and success, is claimed as a mental territory that can then be returned to. The scene of writing is the center of the story Boland relates, but it is a story of invisibility, in a sense, for what occurs within the writer is not visible to us. We can see the product but not its process of becoming. Thus the woman at a desk reading or writing her way into the world makes her first viable poetry. And while we cannot "see" the workings of her mind, we are greeted continually with a narrative of her own progression in context. But what goes on in the act of writing is never fully accounted for, and it is that act of writing, of writing as transforming the writer, that Boland addresses and that she can never entirely represent. Thus her romance with the younger self and the initiate writer in the annunciatory moments of finding one's range, one's interests, one's linguistic adventures would seem most fully crisis-born, and in its first crises of struggling into being, hardly perceptible.

I turn to Boland's repeated story in my afterword to put forward a scene of making and claiming. A poet claims her place and defends it repeatedly. Charles Bernstein in *A Poetics* writes, "What poetry belabors is more important than what poetry says."[5] In some senses, the strong poem holds within it some element of innocence or the ignorance of "error," to extend upon Carson's argument in "Essay On What I Think About Most" in another way. The poets discussed here, somewhat like Boland, return to founding dramas. In Niedecker's poetry, defensive measures literalize water imagery to create a poetry that reflects sensory dissolution. Bishop may seem an accessible poet, and yet her founding images open into nonsense as defense. In Glück, defensive measures recur through the first dramas of rejection, including rejection of a speaker's earlier formulations about herself. In Carson we see a drama of abandonment as a problematic kernel in forms of writing that move across generic boundaries but reassert the existence of a young woman's psychic wound that must be protected (and unhealed so that it can be felt—and serve as a renewable source for contemplation).

In Niedecker the authority of a working-class experience near water, the diurnal cast in one location, a Wisconsin peninsula, is conditioned by sensory vulnerability that marks her language and contributes to her distinctiveness as a poet. The condensing that she engages in repeatedly is part of her self-identity. It is also the primary action in her own enactment of a scene of writing. In Bishop the authority of observation during travel or in an alien environment protects a social self at odds with accepted orders of meaning. The poems evince a retreat from the most "common sense," that is, from the consensus of groups. In Glück the authority of foreknowledge, a perception of fated humanity, is constructed to protect the very stubborn desire to imagine values beyond the ordinary. In Carson the authority of scholarly procedures and the accrual of knowledge is put to service in an erotic yearning that defies completion and invites repetition.

Often the claims a poet makes for poetry are not static but evolve over the course of a career. In the strongest contemporary poets, the most exciting poetry would outpace the writer's prose claims. Niedecker claims for poetry the power to enact the dissolutions of the senses. Her poems operate not only to represent the medium of water but the transporting and transfiguring potentials we attribute to fluids. Amid the poems of "For Paul and Other Poems" is a portion that suggests in concentrated form her own drama in positioning herself as a writer:

> I sit in my own house
> secure,
> follow winter break-up
> thru window glass.
> Ice cakes
> glide downstream
> the wild swans
> of our day.[6]

The house, the passing scene, the seasonal act with its break in earlier routine, the focus on the contemporary: these are the initiatory ingredients for a self that inscribes places with dissolution. Niedecker is a poet of the "break-up" of a scene, the dissolving of the visual as much as the provisional constitution of the visual. Yet the speaker herself is notably "secure" in this act of observation, casting about for language. The speaker encloses her reference to wild swans, inflected through Yeats, in a defense of the local, of her place and time and, in turn, in defense of instability. The poem melts, as Robert Frost would say, on its own making. The ice becomes ice cakes—the domestic "cakes," which are then the smoothly moving actualities "of our day." The season must dissolve, the glass must pointedly be "window glass," sight must be inherently troubled (what is witnessed is witnessed through two panes—eyeglasses and window glasses, for Niedecker). The details must arrive in all their dailiness to glide through time to new readers.

Elizabeth Bishop's affection for oddity can seem like an ingratiating quirkiness. (We should recall that it was difficult for years to pry her reputation from Marianne Moore's shadow, despite what we now readily see as obvious differences between them.) In her poetry Bishop opens a fine crack in sense—and she reminds us that what is taken for granted is a mystery that we cannot entirely absorb. We can even think of Bishop's "The Imaginary Iceberg," the second poem in *North & South* (1946), as a key poem of defense. The iceberg is a giant defensive body that self-ornaments, she tells us, from within. Finally the iceberg proves to be a sublime figure of allegiance, an imagined body that sharpens sight: distant, unapproachable, and preferable: "fleshed, fair, erected indivisible." Art is a construction that tempts us toward but ultimately defies any absolute vision. The poem is the marking of a choice—an observation that is in some ways fanciful and transformative. For all her surface clarities and attention to visual detail, Bishop is not quite within the conventions of poetic realism. She claims for poetry the allurements of nonsense. The poems' lines of defense, broken and permeable, contest common sense. The iceberg is untouchable, but nevertheless we find ourselves compelled by its forbidden vistas. While Niedecker deals in ice cakes and Bishop in icebergs, both poets are nonetheless situating themselves as preoccupied with the way a poem is assembled as a structure and the way that structure cannot ultimately be contained.

Louise Glück's defensive strategies focus in some measures on resisting inherited ideas and sentimentalities. Her early "All Hallows" performs as a defense of poetry and its processes. The poet is supplicant, the landscape uncertain, the time period cast beyond any actual era but instead sheltered in a fairy tale vista, and the spirit is akin to animal life and must be summoned: "And the soul creeps out of the tree."[7] The poem initiates us into her stance as the poet who waits, as a supplicant surely, but finally a successful petitioner, for in "All Hallows" the feral-like creeper is one she beholds and that she has called for. She enacts her own coming-into-power as a poet in this early poem as a scene of fulfillment, but not without a sinister overlay, as if a sort of death tax were to be demanded of the young poet discovering her power.

Carson claims for poetry a wide field in the language and practices of scholarship inflected through erotic obsession. The romantic deceptions she explores accrue particular complexity, for the one deceived comes to expect deception, and in fact seems to be given an education in deception. The beloved is, at least, reliably dishonest. Carson's attraction to scholarship has evolved into a poetic practice, and her attempt to probe the livingness of the erotic and the forces of obsession reanimate ancient conceptions of fruitful error. In "First Chaldaic Oracle" Carson would unpeel language, which cannot be a thing, an object, but a process. Nominalizing, turning nouns into verbs (*cherrying, Praguing*), is here the practice of the scholar who, paradoxically, works to defeat her own habits, to hold up for investigation her tendency to replicate theory and the expected, in order to work toward "That thing you should know. / Because it is out there (orchid) outside your *and*, it is."[8] The parenthesis, the near homage to Wallace Stevens, the verbal play: all suggest a method that takes into account nonaggressive maneuvers of thinking toward, rather than any assumption of possessing, the poem. The poem advocates defense through its own practices; poetry is "That thing you should know"—and as such it is open to processes that have been developed for scholarship; the distinction splitting of knowledge fields can be entered into in poetry, with latitude. And yet the inherent triumphalism of much scholarship is subverted by the drama of a poetic that militates against possession, that makes nouns into processes (including nouns of nature and proper nouns). The poet's scene of writing is a scene that cannot be completed. Research never stops.

The principal action in each of the poems just cited is telling: what glides in Niedecker; what proves untouchable but alluring to touch in Bishop as structures rise in imaginative placement; what creeps in Glück; and what leans forward in both Glück and Carson; and finally in Carson what would take the noun into the realm of the verb. In these four poets an energetic evasiveness would seem part of the very structure of defense. As Marjorie Perloff points out, "The dominant poetic of the American sixties [was] a poetic . . . of strenuous authenticity, the desire to present a self as natural, as organic, and as unmediated as possible."[9] This poetic has lasted up to and will no doubt last beyond our day in part for the illusion of immediacy that it offers. Initially Bishop and Glück could be seen as participating in some aspects of this aesthetic. Yet it becomes far more clear over time that, like Niedecker and Carson, Bishop and Glück share a practice that results in a poetry asserting its defensive difference from an organic, "unmediated" rhetoric in favor of a poetry that is profoundly aware of its artifice and its separateness from what Glück has already dissected as the failures of "sincerity." Nevertheless, I should note here that all four poets' work speaks, no matter what critical/theoretical models are employed, of intense human loneliness. The poets defend against loneliness, but it emerges as a tonal template. The sediment of personality leaks into the poem; the manipulation of codes and conventions cannot abrade personality. The Mother Goose rhymes born out of anonymity that Niedecker has been repeatedly aligned with nevertheless convey the flavor of origin, and Carson's poems with their explicit treatment of sexual betrayal convey the complexity of a remembered identity that is returned to repeatedly.

In reflecting on how poems end or fail to create an ending, Giorgio Agamben remarks that it appears "As if the poem as a formal structure would not and could not end, as if the possibility of the end were radically withdrawn from it, since the end would imply a poetic impossibility: the exact coincidence of sound and sense. At the point in which sound is about to be ruined in the abyss of sense, the poem looks for shelter in suspending its own end in a declaration, so to speak, of the state of poetic emergency."[10] What we don't finish may remain as a summons to us. Poetry is the genre that keeps defending itself by bringing before us charged intimations of not only what might enter language as newly visible but what may not, of what may be speakable and of what may resist speech. However bold, poetry cannot entirely conceal its own avoidances.

Notes

INTRODUCTION: POETRY AS DEFENSE

1. Plato, "from *The Republic: Book X*," in *Criticism: Major Statements*, 4th ed., ed. Charles Kaplan and William Davis Anderson, trans. Benjamin Jowett (Boston: Bedford/St. Martin's, 2000), 14.

2. Wallace Stevens, "Materia Poetica," in *Wallace Stevens: Collected Poetry and Prose*, ed. Frank Kermode and Joan Richardson (New York: Library of America, 1997), 918.

3. Sir Philip Sidney, *The Defense of Poesy*, ed. Albert S. Cook (Boston: Ginn, 1890), 58.

4. Shelley, *A Defense of Poetry*, ed. Albert S. Cook (Boston: Ginn, 1891), 37.

5. Ralph Waldo Emerson, "The Poet," in *The Collected Works of Ralph Waldo Emerson*, vol. III, ed. Joseph Slater (Cambridge: Harvard University Press, 1983), 18.

6. Walter Pater, "From *Studies in the History of the Renaissance, 1888*," in *Criticism: Major Statements*, 4th ed., ed. Charles Kaplan and William Davis Anderson (Boston: St. Martin's, 2000), 357.

7. W. H. Auden, "Making, Knowing, and Judging," in *The Dyer's Hand and Other Essays* (New York: Random, 1962), 60.

8. Lucy McDiarmid, *Auden's Apologies for Poetry* (Princeton: Princeton University Press, 1990), 13.

9. Tristan Tzara, "The Dada Manifesto, 1918," in *Theater of the Avant-Garde 1890–1950*, ed. Bert Cardullo and Robert Knopf (New Haven: Yale University Press, 2001), 284.

10. Marianne Moore, "Poetry," in *The Poems of Marianne Moore*, ed. Grace Schulman (New York: Viking), 2003), 408.

11. Charles Bernstein, *A Poetics* (Cambridge: Harvard University Press, 1992), 1.

12. Emily Dickinson, "The Soul selects her own Society—," in *The Complete Poems of Emily Dickinson*, ed. Thomas H. Johnson (Boston: Little, 1960), 143.

13. See Charles Olson, "Projective Verse," in *Collected Prose: Charles Olson,*, ed. Donald Allen and Benjamin Friedlander (Berkeley: University of California Press, 1997), 239–49.

14. Harold Bloom, "Freud's Concepts of Defense and the Poetic Will," in *The Literary Freud: Mechanisms of Defense and the Poetic Will*, ed. Joseph H. Smith (New Haven: Yale University Press, 1980), 6.

15. Margaret W. Ferguson, *Trials of Desire: Renaissance Defenses of Poetry* (New Haven: Yale University Press, 1983), 5.

16. Margaret W. Ferguson, "Border Territories of Defense: Freud and Defenses of Poetry," in *Literary Freud: Mechanisms of Defense and the Poetic Will* (New Haven: Yale University Press, 1980), 155.

17. Charles Bernstein, *With Strings* (Chicago: University of Chicago Press, 2001), xi.

18. Cary Nelson, *The Incarnate Word: Literature as Verbal Space* (Urbana: University of Illinois Press, 1973), 3.

19. Ibid., 4.

20. Ibid., 5.

21. Bernstein, "Artifice of Absorption," in *A Poetics*, 9.

22. Ibid., 29–30.

23. Daniel Tiffany, *Toy Medium: Materialism and Modern Lyric* (Berkeley: University of California Press, 2000), 15.

24. Moore's lines are quoted as illustrative by Randall Jarrell in "Her Shield" in *Poetry and The Age* (New York: Knopf, 1953), 199.

25. Jarrell, "Her Shield," 198.

26. Ibid., 199.

27. Elisa New, *The Regenerate Lyric: Theology and Innovation in American Poetry* (Cambridge: Cambridge University Press, 1993), 8–9.

28. Susan Stewart, *Poetry and the Fate of the Senses* (Chicago: University of Chicago Press, 2002), 2.

29. Rachel Blau DuPlessis, "Lorine Niedecker, the Anonymous: Gender, Class, Genre and Resistances," in *Lorine Niedecker: Woman & Poet*, ed. Jenny Penberthy (Orono, Maine: National Poetry Foundation, 1996), 113–37.

30. Marjorie Perloff, *Radical Artifice: Writing Poetry in the Age of Media* (Chicago: University of Chicago Press, 1991), 3.

31. Charles Olson, "Projective Verse," in *Collected Prose: Charles Olson,*, 243.

32. Viktor Shklovsky, *Theory of Prose*, trans. Benjamin Sher (Elmwood Park, Il: Dalkey Archive, 1990), 15.

CHAPTER 1: HUMILITY DOES NOT CANCEL STUBBORNNESS: DEFENSIVE POSITIONING IN LORINE NIEDECKER

1. Donald Davie, "Niedecker," *Parnassus* 14, no. 1 (1987): 202.

2. Ibid., 203.

3. Ibid., 207.

4. Ibid., 201.

5. Jenny Penberthy, *Niedecker and the Correspondence with Zukofsky: 1931–1970* (Cambridge: Cambridge University Press, 1993), 3.

6. Niedecker's admiration of Zukofsky as a poet, apparently always sincere, may have been maintained in part because she could hold to a certain aesthetic of difference, which allowed her to appreciate his work without being absorbed into his aesthetic. The further we are from the inception of her work, the clearer her distance from Zukofsky seems, for Niedecker takes William Carlos Williams's focus on the local and lives it on multiple levels, even while resisting representa-

tion through her dissolution of images. Zukofsky, whatever the value he placed upon her as a writer, is as much a witness to her own development as she is to his throughout their friendship.

It may be important to remember that *friend* is a word given unusual emphasis in Niedecker's poetry. It may be placed at points of emphasis within lines or it may occupy an entire line as a single word or be part of a collection's title (*My Friend Tree*). The word is usually held out without irony. The understanding of loneliness in the poems seems undiluted; the meaning of friendship wholly sincere.

7. Rachel Blau DuPlessis, "Lorine Niedecker, the Anonymous: Gender, Class, Genre and Resistances," in *Lorine Niedecker: Woman & Poet*, ed. Jenny Penberthy (Orono, Maine: National Poetry Foundation, 1996), 118.

8. Niedecker, letter to Zukofsky (December 25, 1947), *Niedecker and the Correspondence with Zukofsky: 1931–1970*, ed. Jenny Penberthy (Cambridge: Cambridge University Press, 1993), #18, 146.

9. Richard Caddel, "Consider: Lorine Niedecker and the Environment," in *Lorine Niedecker: Woman & Poet*, 286.

10. Niedecker's letter is quoted in *"Between Your House and Mine": The Letters of Lorine Niedecker to Cid Corman, 1960 to 1970*, ed. Lisa Pater Faranda (Durham: Duke University Press, 1986), 9.

11. Peter Quartermain, "Reading Niedecker," in *Woman & Poet*, 226.

12. DuPlessis, "Lorine Niedecker, the Anonymous," in *Woman & Poet*, 122.

13. Peter Nicholls, "Lorine Niedecker: Rural Surreal," in *Woman & Poet*, 217.

14. Niedecker, letter to Cid Corman (May 13, 1963), in *"Between Your House and Mine,"* 39.

15. Lorine Niedecker, "Traces of Living Things," in *Lorine Niedecker: Collected Works*, ed. Jenny Penberthy (Berkeley: University of California Press, 2002), 239. All poems I have quoted by Niedecker are from this collection, and their page numbers will be cited parenthetically in the text.

16. Niedecker, letter to Cid Corman (February 18, 1962), in *"Between Your House and Mine,"* 33.

17. Penberthy, "Life and Writing," in *Lorine Niedecker: Collected Works*, 2.

18. Ibid., 6.

19. Niedecker, letter to Ronald Ellis (December 24, 1966), in *Lorine Niedecker: Woman & Poet*, 97.

20. Louis Zukofsky, "Comment," *Poetry* 37, no. 4 (1931): 273.

21. Ibid., 276.

22. Ibid., 268.

23. Rachel Blau DuPlessis and Peter Quartermain, "Introduction," in *Objectivist Nexus: Essays in Cultural Poetics*, ed. Rachel Blau DuPlessis and Peter Quartermain (Tuscaloosa: University of Alabama Press, 1999), 3.

24. Ibid., 10.

25. Ibid., 13.

26. Penberthy, *Lorine Niedecker: Collected Works*, 14.

27. Peter Nicholls, "Lorine Niedecker: Rural Surreal," in *Lorine Niedecker: Woman & Poet*, 200.

28. Niedecker, letter to Mary Hoard (introduced as from the "mid-1930s"), in *Lorine Niedecker: Woman and Poet*, 87.

29. Penberthy, "Introduction, in *Niedecker and the Correspondence with Zukofsky*, 73.

30. Gilbert Sorrentino, "Misconstruing Lorine Niedecker," in *Woman & Poet*, 289.

31. Charles Altieri, "The Objectivist Tradition," in *The Objectivist Nexus*, 30.

32. DuPlessis, "Lorine Niedecker, the Anonymous," in *Woman & Poet*, 114.

33. Niedecker, letter to Mary Hoard, in *Woman & Poet*, 88.

34. Nicholls, "Lorine Niedecker: Rural Surreal," in *Woman & Poet*, 193–194.

35. Penberthy, editorial note, in *Lorine Niedecker: Collected Works*, 383.

36. Penberthy, "Life & Writing," in *Lorine Niedecker: Collected Works*, 8.

37. Marjorie Perloff, "L. Before P.: Writing 'For Paul' For Louis," in *Woman & Poet*, 170.

38. Penberthy, *Lorine Niedecker: Collected Works*, 386, see note.

39. Davie, "Niedecker," 207.

40. Martha Nussbaum, *Upheavals of Thought* (Cambridge: Cambridge University Press, 2001), 22.

41. Ibid., 23.

42. Niedecker, letter to Zukofsky (March 16, 1948), in *Niedecker's Correspondence with Zukofsky*, 146.

43. Niedecker, letter to Morgan Gibson (March 7, 1970), in *Woman & Poet*, 93.

CHAPTER 2. TILTING AT SENSE: DEFENSIVE NONSENSE IN ELIZABETH BISHOP

1. Joanne Feit Diehl, "Bishop's Sexual Politics," in *Elizabeth Bishop: The Geography of Gender*, ed. Marilyn May Lombardi (Charlottesville: University Press of Virginia, 1993), 25.

2. Gertrude Stein. "Composition as Explanation," in *Selected Writings of Gertrude Stein*, ed. Carl Van Vechten (New York: Random, 1946), 453.

3. James Fenton notices this resemblance too, in *The Strength of Poetry* (New York: Farrar, Straus, 2001), 139.

4. William Benton, ed., *Exchanging Hats: Elizabeth Bishop's Paintings* (New York: Farrar, Straus, 1996), xviii.

5. Vernon Shetley, *After the Death of Poetry: Poet and Audience in Contemporary Poetry* (Durham: Duke University Press, 1993), 62–63.

6. Bishop, "Seascape," *Elizabeth Bishop: The Complete Poems, 1927–1979* (New York: Farrar, Straus, 1980), 40. Quotations from Bishop's poetry are derived from *The Complete Poems* and will be cited parenthetically.

7. Bishop, "Influences," *American Poetry Review* 14, no. 1 (1985): 15.

8. Denise Riley, *The Words of Selves: Identification, Solidarity, Irony* (Stanford: Stanford University Press, 2000), 73.

9. Paul H. Fry, *A Defense of Poetry: Reflections on the Occasion of Writing* (Stanford: Stanford University Press, 1995), 4.

10. Susan Stewart, *Nonsense: Aspects of Intertextuality in Folklore and Literature* (Baltimore: Johns Hopkins University Press, 1979), 3.

11. Anne Stevenson, *Elizabeth Bishop* (New York: Twayne, 1966), 31.

12. Helen Vendler, "Domestication, Domesticity, and the Otherworldly," in *Elizabeth Bishop and Her Art*, ed. Lloyd Schwartz and Sybil P. Estess (Ann Arbor: University of Michigan Press, 1983), 33.

13. Eavan Boland, "An Un-Romantic American," *Parnassus: Poetry in Review* 14, no. 2 (1988): 88.

14. Thomas Byrom, *Nonsense and Wonder: The Poems and Cartoons of Edward Lear* (New York: Dutton, 1977), 119.

15. Vendler, "Domestication," in *Elizabeth Bishop and her Art*, 32.

16. Edward Lear, "The Pobble who has no toes," *The Complete Verse and Other Nonsense*, ed. Vivian Noakes (London: Penguin, 2001), 398.

17. Stewart, *Nonsense*, 209.

18. Jeredith Merrin, "Elizabeth Bishop: Gaiety, Gayness, and Change," in *Elizabeth Bishop: The Geography of Gender*, 165.

19. Ibid., 166.

20. Marilyn May Lombardi, "The Closet of Breath: Elizabeth Bishop, Her Body and Her Art," in *Elizabeth Bishop: The Geography of Gender*, 47.

21. Ibid., 56.

22. Bishop, "Influences," 16.

23. Lear, "'How pleasant to know Mr Lear!,'" in *The Complete Verse and Other Nonsense*, 429.

24. Robert Lowell, letter to Bishop (August 15, 1957), in *One Art: Letters*, ed. Robert Giroux (New York: Farrar, Straus, 1994), 345.

25. Sandra Gilbert and Susan Gubar, *No Man's Land: The Place of the Woman Writer in the Twentieth Century, vol I: The War of the Words* (New Haven: Yale University Press, 1988), 212.

26. Edward Lear, "Cold are the crabs that crawl on yonder hill," in *The Complete Verse and Other Nonsense*, 386.

27. Susan Stewart, *On Longing: Narratives of the Miniature, the Gigantic, the Souvenir, the Collection* (Durham: Duke University Press, 1993), 171.

28. Robert Pinsky, "The Idiom of a Self: Elizabeth Bishop and Wordsworth," in *Elizabeth Bishop and her Art*, 49.

29. Joanne Feit Diehl, "Bishop's Sexual Politics," in *Elizabeth Bishop: The Geography of Gender*, 33.

30. Alison Rieke, *The Senses of Nonsense* (Iowa City: University of Iowa Press, 1992), 3.

31. John Ashbery, Review of *The Complete Poems*, by Elizabeth Bishop. *Elizabeth Bishop and Her Art*, 202.

32. Helen Vendler, *The Music of What Happen: Poems, Poets, Critics* (Cambridge: Harvard University Press, 1988), 285.

33. Bishop, letter to Marianne Moore (April 4, 1934), in *One Art*, 20.

34. David Kalstone, *Becoming a Poet: Elizabeth Bishop with Marianne Moore and Robert Lowell* (Ann Arbor: University of Michigan Press, 2001), 16.

35. Elizabeth Bishop, letter to Robert Lowell (February 27, 1970), in *One Art*, 515.

36. C. K. Doreski, *Elizabeth Bishop: The Restraints of Language* (Oxford: Oxford University Press, 1993), 41.

CHAPTER 3. EROTIC DISTANCES: DEFENSIVE ELEVATIONS IN LOUISE GLÜCK

1. Louise Glück, "Education of the Poet," *Proofs & Theories* (Hopewell, NJ: Ecco, 1994), 9.

2. Glück, "On George Oppen," in *Proofs & Theories*, 29.

3. Gluck, "Education of the Poet," in *Proofs & Theories*, 10.

4. Nick Halpern, *Everyday and Prophetic: The Poetry of Lowell, Ammons, Merrill, and Rich* (Madison: University of Wisconsin Press, 2003), 240.

5. Brian Henry, "Louise Glück's Monumental Narcissism," *Contemporary Poetry Review*, April 13, 2002 *http://www.cprw.com/henry/gluck.html*.

6. See Lee Upton's *The Muse of Abandonment: Origin, Identity, Mastery in Five American Poets* (Lewisburg: Bucknell University Press, 1998), 119–43.

7. Robert Pinsky, *Democracy, Culture and the Voice of Poetry* (Princeton: Princeton University Press, 2002), 39.

8. Glück, *The Seven Ages* (Hopewell, NJ: Ecco, 2001), 67. Hereafter this collection will be referred to as *SA,* and page numbers will be cited parenthetically in the text.

9. Glück, "The Idea of Courage," in *Proofs & Theories*, 27.

10. Ibid.

11. Glück, quoted in "Gluck to Be Poet Laureate; Won Pulitzer Prize in '93," by Linton Weeks, *The Washington Post,* http://www.washingtonpost.com/wp-dn/articles/A59001–2003Aug28.html.

12. Glück, quoted in "Chronicler of Private Moments Is Named Poet Laureate," by Elizabeth Olson, *The New York Times*, http://www.nytimes.com/2003/08/29/national29POET.html.

13. Glück, "The Forbidden," in *Proofs & Theories*, 53–54.

14. Glück, "On Impoverishment," in *Proofs & Theories*, 134.

15. Glück, "The Best American Poetry 1993," in *Proofs & Theories*, 93.

16. Elizabeth Dodd, *The Veiled Mirror and the Woman Poet: H.D., Louise Bogan, Elizabeth Bishop, and Louise Glück* (Columbia: University of Missouri Press, 1992), 150.

17. Glück, "On Impoverishment," in *Proofs & Theories*, 134.

18. Glück, "The Idea of Courage," in *Proofs & Theories*, 25.

19. Vernon Shetley, *After the Death of Poetry: Poet and Audience in Contemporary America* (Durham: Duke University Press, 1993),192.

20. Glück, "The Education of the Poet," in *Proofs & Theories*, 7.

21. Dodd, *The Veiled Mirror and the Woman Poet*, 149.

22. Helen Vendler, *The Music of What Happens* (Cambridge: Harvard University Press, 1988), 437.

23. Roberto Calasso, *Literature and the Gods*, trans. Tim Parks (New York: Knopf, 2001), 3.

24. Susan Stewart, *Poetry and the Fate of the Senses* (Chicago: University of Chicago Press, 2002), 116.

25. Glück, "Lamentations," *The First Four Books of Poems* (Hopewell, NJ: Ecco, 1995) 150.

26. Wallace Stevens, "Adagia," in *Collected Poetry and Prose,* ed. Frank Kermode and Joan Richardson (New York: Library of America, 1997), 906.

27. Adam Phillips, *Houdini's Box: The Art of Escape* (Cambridge: Harvard University Press, 2001), 30.

28. Linda Gregerson, "The Sower Against Gardens," *Kenyon Review* 23, no. 1 (Winter 2001): 115.

29. Calvin Bedient, "Man is Altogether Desire?" *Salmagundi* 90–91 (Spring-Summer 1991): 218.

CHAPTER 4: SCHOLARSHIP AND DEBASEMENT: OVERLAYING THE DEFENSES IN ANNE CARSON

1. Anne Carson, "Essay On What I Think About Most," *Men in the Off Hours* (New York: Vintage, 2000), 35. Hereafter this collection will be referred to as *MOH*, and page numbers will be cited parenthetically.

2. Carson, *Eros the Bittersweet* (Normal, IL: Dalkey Archive, 1998), 121.

3. Carson, ibid., 8.

4. Carson, *Economy of the Unlost* (Princeton: Princeton University Press, 1999), viii.

5. Carson, interview with John D'Agata, "A ——— with Anne Carson," *Iowa Review* 27, no. 2 (Summer-Fall 1997), 13.

6. Peter Quartermain, *Disjunctive Poetics: From Gertrude Stein and Louis Zukofsky to Susan Howe* (New York: Cambridge University Press, 1992), 9.

7. Carson, interview with John D'Agata, "A ——— with Anne Carson," 14.

8. Carson, *Eros the Bittersweet*, 145.

9. David C. Ward, "Anne Carson: Addressing the Wound," *PN Review* 27, no. 5 (May-June 2001): 13. In "Carson: Mind and Heart," Mark Halliday hedges his view about Carson's learned poetry: "the erudition could turn out to be (as regards the poetry), upon reflection, more of a flourishing than a nourishing" (*Chicago Review* 45, no. 2 [1999]: 121–27).

10. Ward, "Anne Carson: Addressing the Wound," 16.

11. Carson, interview with Mary Gannon, "Beauty Prefers an Edge," *Poets and Writers* (March/April 2001): 28–29.

12. Carson, ibid., 31.

13. Carson, "The Glass Essay," in *Glass, Irony and God* (New York: New Directions, 1995), 31.

14. Elaine Scarry, *On Beauty and Being Just* (Princeton, NJ: Princeton University Press, 1999), 12.

15. See Carson, *Eros the Bittersweet*, xi.

16. Carson, "The Glass Essay," 11–12.

17. Carson, "The Book of Isaiah," in *Glass, Irony and God*, 112.

18. Carson, *Eros the Bittersweet*, 77.

19. Ibid., 30.

20. Carson, "Dirt and Desire: Essay on the Phenomenology of Female Pollution in Antiquity," in *Men in the Off Hours,* 130.

21. Ibid., 131.

22. Carson, *Eros the Bittersweet*, 16.

23. Ibid, 17.

24. Carson, *Autobiography of Red* (New York: Knopf, 1999), 105.

25. Carson, "The Gender of Sound," in *Glass, Irony and God*, 130.

26. Carson, *Eros the Bittersweet*, 4.

27. Carson, ibid., 169.

28. Carson, *Autobiography of Red*, 43.

29. Carson, *Plainwater: Essays and Poetry* (New York: Vintage, 1995), 223.

30. Carson, "Dirt and Desire," 130.

31. Carson, *Plainwater*, 222.

32. Carson, *Eros the Bittersweet*, 20.

33. Ibid., 21.

34. Ibid., xi.

35. Carson, "Introduction," in *Plainwater*, 29.

36. Carson, *Eros the Bittersweet*, 171.

37. Ibid., 52.

38. Carson, "Beauty Prefers an Edge," in *Poets & Writers*, 32.

39. Ibid., 33.

40. Carson, *Plainwater*, 33.

41. Carson, *The Beauty of the Husband: A Fictional Essay in 29 Tangos* (New York: Alfred A. Knopf, 2001), 9. Hereafter the title of this collection will be abbreviated as *BH*, and page numbers will be cited parenthetically in the text.

42. Scarry, *On Beauty and Being Just*, 52–53.

43. Carson, *Autobiography of Red*, 95.

44. Harriet Zinnes, "What is Time Made Of? The Poetry of Anne Carson," *Hollins Critic* 38, no. 1 (February 2001): 8.

45. Carson, interview with John D'Agata, "A Talk with Anne Carson," *Brick* 57, no. 1 (Fall 1997): 14.

46. Ibid., 21.

47. "Who's Who," in *If Not, Winter: Fragments of Sappho*, ed. and trans. Anne Carson (New York: Knopf, 2002), 384.

AFTERWORD: THE PRICE WE PAY FOR MAKING CLAIMS

1. Elizabeth Bishop, "One Art," in *The Complete Poems* (New York: Farrar, Straus, 1980), 178.

2. Hélène Cixous, *Three Steps on the Ladder of Writing*, trans. Sarah Cornell and Susan Sellers (New York: Columbia University Press, 1993), 156.

3. Eavan Boland, *Object Lessons: The Life of the Woman and the Poet in Our Time* (New York: Norton, 1995), xv–xvi.

4. Helen Vendler, *Coming of Age as a Poet: Milton, Keats, Eliot, Plath* (Cambridge: Harvard University Press, 2003), 4.

5. Charles Bernstein, *A Poetics* (Cambridge: Harvard University Press, 1992), 8.

6. Lorine Niedecker, *Collected Works*, ed. Jenny Penberthy (Berkeley: University of California Press, 2002), 167.

7. Louise Glück, *The First Four Books of Poems* (Hopewell, NJ: Ecco, 1995), 61.

8. Anne Carson, *Men in the Off Hours* (New York: Vintage, 2000), 11.

9. Marjorie Perloff, *Radical Artifice: Writing Poetry in the Age of Media* (Chicago: University of Chicago Press, 1991), 20.

10. Giorgio Agamben, *The End of the Poem*, trans. Daniel Heller-Roazen (Stanford: Stanford University Press, 1999), 113.

Bibliography

Agamben, Giorgio. *The End of the Poem: Studies in Poetics*. Translated by Daniel Heller-Roazen. Stanford: Stanford University Press, 1999.

Altieri, Charles. "The Objectivist Tradition." In *The Objectivist Nexus: Essays in Cultural Poetics*, edited by Rachel Blau DuPlessis and Peter Quartermain, 25–36. Tuscaloosa: University of Alabama Press, 1999.

Ashbery, John. Rev. of *The Complete Poems*, by Elizabeth Bishop. *Elizabeth Bishop and Her Art*. Edited by Lloyd Schwartz and Sybil P. Estess. Ann Arbor: University of Michigan Press, 1983.

Auden, W. H. *The Dyer's Hand and Other Essays*. New York: Random, 1962.

Bedient, Calvin. "Man is Altogether Desire?" In *Salmagundi* 99091 (Spring–Summer 1991): 212–30.

Benton, William. "Introduction." In *Exchanging Hats: Elizabeth Bishop's Paintings*, vii–xx. New York: Farrar, Straus, 1996.

Bernstein, Charles. *A Poetics*. Cambridge, MA: Harvard University Press, 1992.

———. *with strings*. Chicago: University of Chicago Press, 2001.

Bishop, Elizabeth. *The Complete Poems: 1927–1979*. New York: Farrar, 1983.

———. *Exchanging Hats: Elizabeth Bishop Paintings*. Edited by William Benton. New York: Farrar, Straus, 1996.

———. "Influences." *American Poetry Review* 14, no. 1 (1985): 11–16.

———. *One Art: Letters*. Edited by Robert Giroux. New York: Noonday, 1994.

Bloom, Harold. "Freud's Concepts of Dense and the Poetic Will." In *The Literary Freud: Mechanisms of Defense and the Poetic Will*, edited by Joseph H. Smith, 1–28. New Haven: Yale University Press, 1980.

Boland, Eavan. *The Lost Land: Poems*. New York: Norton, 1998.

———. *Object Lessons: The Life of the Poet in Our Time*. New York: Norton, 1995.

———. *An Origin Like Water: Collected Poems 1967–1987*. New York: Norton, 1996.

———. "An Un-Romantic American." *Parnassus: Poetry in Review* 14, no. 2 (1988): 73–92.

Byrom, Thomas. *Nonsense and Wonder: The Poems and Cartoons of Edward Lear*. New York: Dutton, 1977.

Caddel, Richard. "Consider: Lorine Niedecker and the Environment." In *Lorine Niedecker: Woman & Poet*. Edited by Jenny Penberthy, 281–86. Orono, ME: National Poetry Foundation, 1996.

Calasso, Roberto. *Literature and the Gods*. Translated by Tim Parks. New York: Knopf, 2001.

Carson, Anne. *Autobiography of Red: A Novel in Verse*. New York: Knopf, 1999.

———. *The Beauty of the Husband: A Fictional Essay in 29 Tangos*. New York: Knopf, 2001.

———. *Economy of the Unlost (Reading Simonides of Keos with Paul Celan)*. Princeton, NJ: Princeton University Press, 1999.

———. *Eros the Bittersweet*. Dalkey Archive Press, 1998.

———. *Glass, Irony and God*. New York: New Directions, 1995.

———, ed. and trans. *If Not, Winter: Fragments of Sappho*. New York: Knopf, 2002.

———. *Men in the Off Hours*. New York: Vintage, 2000.

———. *Plainwater: Essays and Poetry*. New York: Vintage, 1995.

Cixous, Hélène. *Three Steps on the Ladder of Writing*. Translated by Sarah Cornell and Susan Sellers. New York: Columbia University Press, 1993.

D'Agata, John. "A Talk with Anne Carson." (Interview). *Brick* 57 (Fall 1997): 14–22.

———. "A _____ with Anne Carson." (Interview). *Iowa Review* 17, no. 2 (Summer–Fall 1997): 1–22.

Davie, Donald. "Niedecker." *Parnassus* 14, no. 1 (1987): 201–7.

de Bolla, Peter. *Art Matters*. Cambridge, MA: Harvard University Press, 2001.

Dickie, Margaret and Thomas Travisano. *Gendered Modernisms: American Women Poets and their Readers*. Philadelphia: University of Pennsylvania Press, 1996.

Dickinson, Emily. *The Complete Poems of Emily Dickinson*. Edited by Thomas H. Johnson, Boston: Little, Brown, 1960.

Diehl, Joanne Feit. "Bishop's Sexual Politics." In *Elizabeth Bishop: The Geography of Gender*, edited by Marilyn May Lombardi, 17–45. Charlottesville: University Press of Virginia, 1993.

Dodd, Elizabeth. *The Veiled Mirror and the Woman Poet: H. D., Louise Bogan, Elizabeth Bishop, and Louise Glück*. Columbia: University of Missouri Press, 1992.

Doreski, C. K. *Elizabeth Bishop: The Restraints of Language*. Oxford: Oxford University Press, 1993.

DuPlessis, Rachel Blau, "Lorine Niedecker, the Anonymous: Gender, Class, Genre and Resistances." In *Lorine Niedecker: Woman & Poet*, edited by Jenny Penberthy. 113–37. Orono, ME: National Poetry Foundation, 1996.

Emerson, Ralph Waldo. *The Collected Works of Ralph Waldo Emerson*. Vol. III. Essays: Second Series. Cambridge, MA: Harvard University Press, 1983.

Faranda, Lisa Pater. *"Between Your House and Mine": The Letters of Lorine Niedecker to Cid Corman, 1960 to 1970*. Durham: Duke University Press, 1986.

Fenton, James. *The Strength of Poetry: Oxford Lectures*. New York: Farrar, Straus, 2001.

Ferguson, Margaret W. "Border Territories of Defense: Freud and Defenses of Poetry." In *The Literary Freud: Mechanisms of Defense and the Poetic Will*, edited by Joseph H. Smith, 149–80. New Haven: Yale University Press, 1980.

———. *Trials of Desire: Renaissance Defenses of Poetry*. New Haven: Yale University Press, 1983.

Fry, Paul H. *A Defense of Poetry: Reflections on the Occasion of Writing*. Stanford: Stanford University Press, 1995.

Gannon, Mary. "Anne Carson: Beauty Prefers an Edge." Interview with Anne Carson. *Poets & Writers* 29, no. 2 (March/April 2001): 26–33.

Gilbert, Sandra M. and Susan Gubar. *No Man's Land: The Place of the Woman Writer in the Twentieth Century*. Vol 1: The War of the Words. New Haven: Yale University Press, 1988.

Glück, Louise. *Ararat*. New York: Ecco, 1990.

———. *Descending Figure*. New York Ecco, 1980.

———. *Firstborn*. New York: New American Library, 1968.

———. *The First Four Books of Poems*. Hopewell, NJ: Ecco, 1995.

———. *Meadowlands*. Hopewell, NJ: Ecco, 1996.

———. *Proofs & Theories*. Hopewell, NJ: Ecco, 1994.

———. *The Seven Ages*. Hopewell, NJ: Ecco, 200l.

———. *The Triumph of Achillles*. New York: Ecco, 1985.

———. *Vita Nova*. Hopewell, NJ: Ecco, 1999.

———. *The Wild Iris*. Hopewell, NJ: Ecco, 1992.

Gregerson, Linda. "The Sower Against Gardens." *Kenyon Review* 23, no. 1 (Winter 2001): 115–33.

Halliday, Mark. "Carson: Mind and Heart." *Chicago Review* 45, no. 2 (1999): 121–27.

Halpern, Nick. *Everyday and Prophetic: The Poetry of Lowell, Ammons, Merrill, and Rich*. Madison: University of Wisconsin Press, 2003.

Henry, Brian. "Louise Glück's Monumental Narcissism." *Contemporary Poetry Review*, April 13, 2002. http://www.cprw.com/henry/gluck.html.

Jarrell, Randall. *Poetry and the Age*. New York: Knopf, 1953.

Johnson, Barbara. *The Feminist Difference: Literature, Psychoanalysis, Race, and Gender*. Cambridge: Harvard University Press, 1998.

Kalstone, David. *Becoming a Poet: Elizabeth Bishop with Marianne Moore and Robert Lowell*. Ann Arbor: University of Michigan Press, 2001.

Lear, Edward. *The Complete Verse and Other Nonsense*. Edited by Vivian Noakes. London: Penguin, 2001.

Lombardi, Marilyn May. "The Closet of Breath: Elizabeth Bishop, Her Body and Her Art." In *Elizabeth Bishop: The Geography of Gender*, edited by Marilyn May Lombardi, 46–69. Charlottesville: University Press of Virginia, 1993.

McCabe, Susan. *Elizabeth Bishop: Her Poetics of Loss*. University Park: Pennsylvania State University Press, 1994.

McDiarmid, Lucy. *Auden's Apologies for Poetry*. Princeton: Princeton University Press, 1990.

Merrin, Jeredith. "Elizabeth Bishop: Gaiety, Gayness, and Change. In *Elizabeth Bishop: The Geography of Gender*, edited by Marilyn May Lombardi, 153–72. Charlottesville: University Press of Virginia, 1993.

Moore, Marianne. *The Poems of Marianne Moore*. Edited by Grace Schulman. New York: Viking, 2003.

Moramarco, Fred and William Sullivan. *Containing Multitudes: Poetry in the United States Since 1950*. New York: Twayne, 1998.

Nelson, Cary. *The Incarnate Word: Literature as Verbal Space*. Urbana: University of Illinois Press, 1973.

New, Elisa. *The Line's Eye: Poetic Experience, American Sight*. Cambridge, MA: Harvard University Press, 1998.

Nicholls, Peter. "Lorine Niedecker: Rural Surreal." In *Lorine Niedecker: Woman & Poet*, 193–217. Orono, Maine: National Poetry Foundation, 1996.

Niedecker, Lorine. *Collected Works*. Edited by Jenny Penberthy. Berkeley: University of California Press, 2002.

———. *From This Condensery*. Edited by Robert J. Bertholf. East Haven, CT: Jargon, 1985.

———. *The Granite Pail: The Selected Poems of Lorine Niedecker*. Edited by Cid Corman. San Francisco: North Point, 1985.

Nussbaum, Martha. *Upheavals of Thought*. Cambridge: Cambridge University Press, 2001.

Olson, Charles. *Collected Prose: Charles Olson*. Edited by Donald Allen and Benjamin Friedlander. Berkeley: University of California Press, 1997.

Olson, Elizabeth. "Chronicler of Private Moments Is Named Poet Laureate." *The New York Times*, http://www.nytimes.com/2003/08/29/national29POET.html.

Pater, Walter. "From *Studies in the History of the Renaissance*, 1888." In *Criticism: Major Statements*, 4th ed., edited by Charles Kaplan and William David Anderson, 354–57. Boston: St. Marin's, 2000.

Penberthy, Jenny. "Life and Writing." In *Lorine Niedecker: Collected Works*. Berkeley: University of California Press, 2002.

———, ed. *Lorine Niedecker: Woman and Poet*. Orono, ME: National Poetry Foundation, 1996.

———, ed. *Niedecker and the Correspondence with Zukofsky 1931–1970*. Cambridge: Cambridge University Press, 1993.

Perloff, Marjorie. "L. Before P.: Writing 'For Paul' For Louis." In *Lorine Niedecker: Woman & Poet*, 157–70. Orono, ME: National Poetry Foundation, 1996.

———. *Radical Artifice: Writing Poetry in the Age of Media*. Chicago: University of Chicago Press, 1991.

Phillips, Adam. *Houdini's Box: The Art of Escape*. New York: Pantheon, 2001.

Pinsky, Robert. *Democracy, Culture and the Voice of Poetry*. Princeton, NJ: Princeton University Press, 2002.

———. "The Idiom of a Self: Elizabeth Bishop and Wordsworth." In *Elizabeth Bishop and Her Art*, edited by Lloyd Schwartz and Sybil P. Estess, 49–60. Ann Arbor: University of Michigan Press, 1983.

Plato. "from *The Republic: Book X*." In *Criticism: Major Statements*, 4th ed., edited by Charles Kaplan and William Davis, translated by Benhamin Jowett, 14. Boston: Bedford/St. Martin's, 2000.

Quartermain, Peter. *Disjunctive Poetics: From Gertrude Stein and Louis Zukofsky to Susan Howe*. Cambridge, MA: Cambridge University Press, 1992.

———. "Reading Niedecker." In *Lorine Niedecker: Woman & Poet*, 219–27. Orono, ME: National Poetry Foundation, 1996.

Rieke, Alison. *The Senses of Nonsense*. Iowa City: University of Iowa Press, 1992.

Riley, Denise. *The Words of Selves: Identification, Solidarity, Irony*. Stanford: Stanford University Press, 2000.

Sappho. *If Not, Winter: Fragments of Sappho*. Translated by Anne Carson. New York: Knopf, 2002.

Scarry, Elaine. *On Beauty and Being Just*. Princeton, NJ: Princeton University Press, 1999.

Scroggins, Mark. *Louis Zukofsky and the Poetry of Knowledge*. Tuscaloosa: University of Alabama Press, 1998.

Shelley. *A Defense of Poetry*. Edited by Albert S. Cook. Boston: Ginn, 1891.

Shetley, Vernon. *After the Death of Poetry: Poet and Audience in Contemporary America*. Durham: Duke University Press, 1992.

Shklovsky, Viktor. *Theory of Prose*. Translated by Benjamin Sher. Elmwood Park, IL: Dalkey, 1990.

Sidney, Sir Philip. *The Defense of Poesy*. Edited by Albert S. Cook. Boston: Ginn, 1890.

Smith, Joseph H. *The Literary Freud: Mechanisms of Defense and Poetic Will*. New Haven: Yale University Press, 1980.

Smith, Stevie. *Collected Poems*. Edited by James MacGibbon. New York: New Directions, 1983.

Sorrentino, Gilbert. "Misconstruing Lorine Niedecker." In *Lorine Niedecker: Woman & Poet*, 287–92. Orono, ME: National Poetry Foundation, 1996.

Stein, Gertrude. "Composition as Explanation." In *Selected Writings of Gertrude Stein*. Edited by Carl Van Vechten, 453–61. New York: Random, 194.

Stevens, Wallace. *Collected Poetry and Prose*. Edited by Frank Kermode and Joan Richardson. New York: Library of America, 1997.

Stevenson, Anne. *Elizabeth Bishop*. New York: Twayne, 1966.

Stewart, Susan. *Nonsense: Aspects of Intertexuality in Folklore and Literature*. Baltimore: Johns Hopkins, 1979.

———. *On Longing: Narratives of the Miniature, the Gigantic, the Souvenir, the Collection*. Durham: Duke University Press, 1993.

———. *Poetry and the Fate of the Senses*. Chicago: University of Chicago Press, 2002.

Tiffany, Daniel. *Toy Medium: Materialism and Modern Lyric*. Berkeley University of California Press, 2000.

Tzara, Tristan. "Dada Manifesto, 1918." In *Theater of the Avant-Garde, 1890–1950: A Critical Anthology*, edited by Bert Cardullo and Robert Knopf, 283–89. New Haven: Yale, 2001.

Upton, Lee. *The Muse of Abandonment: Origin, Identity, Mastery in Five American Poets*. Lewisburg: Bucknell University Press, 1998.

Vendler, Helen. *The Breaking of Style: Hopkins, Heaney, Graham*. Cambridge: Harvard University Press, 1995.

———. *Coming of Age as a Poet: Milton, Keats, Eliot, Plath*. Cambridge: Harvard University Press, 2003.

———. "Domestication, Domesticity, and the Otherworldly." In *Elizabeth Bishop and Her Art*, edited by Lloyd Schwartz and Sybil P. Estess, 32–48. Ann Arbor: University of Michigan Press, 1983.

———. "Elizabeth Bishop." In *The Music of What Happens: Poems, Poets, Critics,* 284–99. Cambridge, MA: Harvard University Press, 1988.

———. *The Music of What Happens.* Cambridge: Harvard University Press, 1988.

Ward, David C. "Anne Carson: Addressing the Wound." *PN Review* 27, no. 5 (May–June 2001): 13–16.

Weeks, Linton. "Glück to Be Poet Laureate; Won Pulitzer Prize in '93." *The Washington Post.* http://www.washingtonppost.com/wp-dn/articles/A59001–2003Aug 28.html.

Zinnes, "What is Time Made Of? The Poetry of Anne Carson." *Hollins Critic* 38, no. 1 (February 2001): 1–10.

Zukofsky, Louis. "Comment. Program: 'Objectivists' 1931." *Poetry* 37, no. 5 (February 1931): 268–72.

———, ed. *Poetry* 37, no. 5 (February 1931).

———. "Sincerity and Objectification." *Poetry* 37, no. 5 (February 1931): 272–85.

Index